CULTURAL PERSPECTIVES IN FAMILY THERAPY

James C. Hansen, Editor
Celia Jaes Falicov, Volume Editor

The Family Therapy Collections

AN ASPEN PUBLICATION®

Aspen Systems Corporation
Rockville, Maryland
London
1983

Library of Congress Cataloging in Publication Data
Main entry under title:

Cultural perspectives in family therapy.

(The Family therapy collections, ISSN 0735-9152)
Includes bibliographies and index.
1. Family psychotherapy—Social aspects—Addresses,
essays, lectures, 2. Psychiatry, Transcultural—
Addresses, essays, lectures. I. Hansen, James C.
II. Falicov, Celia Jaes. III. Series. [DNLM:
1. Family therapy. 2. Culture. WM 130.5.F2   C968]
RC488.5.C84   1983   616.89'156   83-8817
ISBN: 0-89443-606-6

Publisher: John Marozsan
Managing Editor: Margot Raphael
Editorial Services: Ruth Judy
Printing and Manufacturing: Debbie Collins

The Family Therapy Collections series is indexed in
Psychological Abstracts and the PsycINFO database.

Library of Congress Catalog Card Number: 83-8817
ISBN: 0-89443-606-6
ISSN: 0735-9152

Printed in the United States of America

1   2   3   4   5

Table of Contents

Board of Editors

Board of Editors
(continued)

Contributors

Volume Editor
CELIA JAES FALICOV

ANA ISABEL ALVAREZ
City College of San Francisco
San Francisco, California

GUILLERMO BERNAL
University of California
San Francisco, California

DOUGLAS BREUNLIN
Institute for Juvenile Research
Chicago, Illinois

LILYAN BRUDNER-WHITE
Adjunct Associate Professor
University of California, Irvine
Irvine, California

BRIAN CADE
The Family Institute
Cardiff, Wales

MAX CORNWELL
University of New South Wales
Sydney, Australia

CELIA JAES FALICOV
University of California, San Diego
San Diego Family Institute
San Diego, California

JAN FAULKNER
Alameda County Mental Health
Services
Oakland, California

MANUEL GUTIERREZ
Aspira, Inc.
Philadelphia, Pennsylvania

GEORGE KITIHARA KICH
Berkeley, California

JAY LAPPIN
Philadelphia Child Guidance Clinic
Philadelphia, Pennsylvania

DAVID McGILL
Smith College
Northampton, Massachusetts

BRAULIO MONTALVO
Philadelphia Child Guidance Clinic
Bryn Mawr College
Philadelphia, Pennsylvania

JOHN SCHWARTZMAN
Center for Family Studies
The Family Institute of Chicago
Institute of Psychiatry
Northwestern Memorial Hospital
and Northwestern University
Medical School
Chicago, Illinois

CARLOS E. SLUZKI
Mental Research Institute
Palo Alto, California
University of California,
San Francisco
San Francisco, California

FROMA WALSH
The Family Institute of Chicago
Center for Family Studies
Northwestern University Medical
School
Chicago, Illinois

Preface

The Family Therapy Collections, published quarterly, are designed primarily for professional practitioners. Each volume contains articles authored by practicing professionals, providing in-depth coverage of a single significant topic of family therapy.

This volume focuses on the cultural dimensions in family therapy. Cultural dimensions involve the historical continuity and psychological identity that affect the thinking, feeling, and behavior of family members. Everyone is a member of a family and every family has an ethnic-cultural heritage. The cultural and ethnic values play a significant role in family behaviors. Many of these values are not consciously held, but seem "natural" to the family.

There is an attempt in this volume not to stereotype families but to examine cultural dimensions that stimulate exploration of each family. A clinician needs to understand each family and its cultural manners. Many families do not come from just one background but are dual culture families. Families have not melted into a homogeneous American culture. Our society is multicultural. To understand the frame of reference of the family, therefore, it is necessary to understand the concepts of the nuclear and extended family.

Cultural dimensions are also involved in the relationship between the family and the therapist. Therapists are influenced by their cultural values. No matter what theoretical approach is used in therapy, therapists must be aware of their own values and seek to understand those of the family. The therapist's focus should move from the large cultural groups to individual families. Excellent case material is provided in this volume to illustrate ideas and help therapists apply anthropological and sociological concepts in therapy.

Dr. Celia Jaes Falicov is the volume editor. Dr. Falicov provides training, supervision, and clinical services at the San Diego Family Institute, and is on the faculty at the University of California at San Diego and the Mental Research Institute in Palo Alto. She completed her psychology studies at the University of Buenos Aires and received a doctorate from the University of Chicago. Before moving to San Diego she directed the Family Systems Program at the Institute for Juvenile Research in Chicago and was on the faculty of the University of Illinois and the Family Institute of Chicago. She has numerous publications in family therapy, many with an emphasis on cultural dimensions. Dr. Falicov has developed a meaningful concept for this volume and selected knowledgeable professionals to write the articles. The result is a stimulating, thought-provoking, and useful volume for the practicing family therapist.

James C. Hansen
Editor
May, 1983

Introduction

Families live. They continue to live in their own variegated ways, producing their variegated effects as they draw selectively on the changing values, norms and opportunities of the society of which they are a part and as they experience selectively the constraints of that society. While living always in a world that builds them, families live also in the worlds they build themselves, as they always have.

Gerald Handel (1967)

Our lives are culture-bound and shaped. Cultural influences are so ubiquitous, they permeate and mold our world views. Psychotherapists witness a broad and varied spectrum of human relationships among their clients. Consideration of these differences implies a recognition of individual and family variety that should rightly precede attempts at generalization. But when those variations are viewed through cultural lenses the field of individual family behaviors undergoes some organizational shifts, like a clustering or patterning effect that allows certain connections to be made and an appreciation of group differences and similarities to emerge. Cultural lenses are constructs that serve to organize complex realities. They can be labeled as social organization, philosophical or belief systems, ethnicity, religion, language, or family values.

Although family therapy has from its inception looked at behavior as contextual, the word ''context'' has been used mainly to refer to the family as the context for individual behavior. Just as individual psychology has focused on individual unique personality factors, family therapy has tended to look at each family as a unique system of interactions, operating within a more-or-less closed small unit, where the behavior of one person becomes the context for the behavior of another person. This concentration on the "interior" of the family has been crucial for the advances in the understanding of family systems, but it has also resulted in a concept of the family mostly regulated by its own private rules and isolated from the larger sociocultural context. In every family, many regularities of behavior certainly stem from idiosyncratic interactions, but other patterns can be associated with sociocultural rules that serve to organize, regulate, maintain, or even change behavior within the family.

Since different cultures and subcultures organize different adaptive family arrangements and interactive styles, an understanding of the sociocultural context becomes crucial for assessing the meaning and function of family behavior. Cultural issues are also present in the family's interactions with other organizations and institutions. The manner in which problems and solutions are perceived, explained, and dealt with; the pathways of seeking and obtaining help; what is expected; and how one interacts with a professional are all affected by cultural and social class factors.

In addition, therapists, too, like families, draw on culturally bound concepts and techniques when evolving a therapeutic context. Regardless of their attempts to respect cultural differences, therapists are hard-put to avoid the use of their own culturally determined models to organize the behaviors they observe. Aside from the personal cultural background of each therapist, the field of family therapy has definite cultural and subcultural values reflected in various theoretical constructs, hypotheses, conventions, and taboos. Since theories unavoidably reflect cultural values, a metatheory— i.e., a theory about theories—or at least, a metaposition about one's theories about families and family therapy, is a necessary perspective.

The incorporation of cultural dimensions in family therapy belongs in the realm of integrative interdisciplinary and ecological enterprise that is in itself an expression of present ideological trends. A recent contribution edited by McGoldrick, Pearce and Giordano (1982) addresses the issue of culture and family therapy by focusing specifically on ethnicity as a powerful force that permeates family life. Their work aims to sensitize the clinician to ethnic factors underlying family behaviors and to provide guidance in selecting ethnically-attuned interventions.

The present volume approaches the issue of cultural dimensions in family therapy from different perspectives. Without underestimating the importance of ethnic roots as the traditional background for shared cultural values, cultural issues are defined here as sets of common adaptive behaviors and experience derived from membership in a variety of different contexts:

ecological setting (rural, urban, suburban), philosophical or religious values, nationality and ethnicity, types of family organization, social class, occupation, migratory patterns and stage of acculturation; or values derived from partaking of similar historical moments or particular ideologies. Thus, cultural differences are seen as tied to different types of group membership or other forms of contextual inclusion or exclusion, not necessarily subsumed under specific ethnic group membership. Since families partake and combine features of several of the contexts, it is necessary for therapists to consider membership in all of the relevant contexts simultaneously.

But how is one to approach the incorporation of these exceedingly complex sets of cultural variables in family therapy theory and practice? What is the actual place of culture in family therapy? When, what for, and how are cultural dimensions to be articulated with the therapeutic context? At this exploratory stage there is a search for an answer to these questions through diverse avenues and viewpoints. Some approaches advocate the need for a priori knowledge of ethnic or other cultural traits (e.g., Italians value very close family ties). Others prefer to focus on universal invariants in families' predicaments (e.g., children need to be raised by adults) and consider cultural differences to be tangential to the therapy situation. There are also many in-between positions. Some stress the need to sensitize therapists to the cultural underpinnings of their own theories and interventions and to modify or develop theories to fit different cultures. Others have begun to search for new concepts and methodologies to detect and make use of cultural values and behaviors as they emerge during the treatment process, and thus rely minimally on a priori knowledge of the particular culture of the family. Each of these approaches affords a different view of cultural issues and helps provide a better understanding of families' and therapists' behaviors, and each is represented in the present volume.

There are also risks to be taken and problems to be resolved when entering this area. This volume implicitly addresses some of these risks and problems. One of the difficulties is that the use of broad generalizations about cultural norms and values learned through anthropology or sociology may be valid at the macrosocial level but always need refinement and qualification at the microsocial level. In fact, when we apply sociocultural norms to individual families we may begin to use stereotypes and clichés that hamper rather than facilitate therapeutic work. It may be equally problematic, however, to ignore cultural norms and expectations when they have relevancy and application to the therapeutic situation in crucial aspects of assessment and intervention.

Including cultural perspectives in family therapy implies an awareness of this dilemma and a constant vigilance in navigating between the Scylla of cultural ethnocentrism that ignores basic cultural differences and uses similar lenses to judge and help all families and the Charybdis of cultural stereotyping that misses crucial individual differences. Like the statistician who starts with a null hypothesis and determines significance in a probabilistic framework, so the family therapist must approach the clinical relevance of cultural issues as a balancing of risks between two errors: underestimating the impact of culture (false positive or Type I error) and incorrectly attributing dysfunction to a pattern that is normative in the family's culture, or overestimating and magnifying the importance of culture at the expense of failing to recognize dysfunctional family processes (false negative or Type II error).* Many of the approaches suggested here maximize the gains of learning to think culturally and by and large minimize the risks of either cultural stereotyping or missing important cultural angles. Furthermore, since these articles approach culture as interconnected with several specific contexts, the risks of introducing linear determination and "blaming the culture" are also lessened.

By their very nature the culture of families and the culture of therapists are in the process of constant transformation. These articles attempt to heed this evolution and avoid reifying issues of cultural content by focusing on issues of organization and process, in the form of models, methodologies, and metatheories. The result is a dynamic, process-oriented view where culture becomes either background or foreground depending on the issue at hand. Culture can also become organizational reality, defensive mask, or powerful myth, allowing the therapeutic choice to emphasize or not, much as one punctuates other issues. And, glimpses of the analogic element inherent in culture can be captured in some of these approaches.

There are many interconnecting threads in this tapestry of statements about family and culture, and these threads could contain the beginnings of a new conceptual and methodological vocabulary for the incorporation of "cultural tools" that can ultimately add complexity and specificity to our understanding and practice of family therapy.

Froma Walsh presents cultural ideologies about normality that prevail in this society and exert a powerful influence on families and therapists alike. Even though these ideologies have become cultural myths that lag behind social realities, Walsh demonstrates their critical relevance to the clinical situation by showing how they influence, often covertly, the ways families

---

*This concept was developed in collaboration with Betty M. Karrer, M.A.

regard themselves and the criteria clinicians use to assess, define objectives, and treat families in distress.

In searching for a perspective for the use of the cultural dimension in family therapy, Braulio Montalvo and Manuel Gutierrez offer their view that first priority should be given to the interinstitutional (and cross-cultural) dilemmas between the family of the minority subculture and the surrounding institutions that appear with invariant regularity particularly during crucial transitions. Issues of ethnic legacy and cultural traditions then are discovered in the interaction with the therapist and can be used either to help get rid of cultural beliefs that hamper adaptation to the harsh socioeconomic reality or to draw upon the culture to expand a family's adaptational repertoire.

Guillermo Bernal and Ana Alvarez stress the need to integrate cultural and socioeconomic factors and propose the use of a model that interrelates the influence of work systems on the family with core ethnocultural values as they evolve across generations. They illustrate the application of their model to the clinical situation through examples of their work with Hispanic families.

Celia Falicov and Lilyan Brudner-White suggest that a central concept in family therapy, the family triangle, needs to be considered from different viewpoints, including a cultural one, before assigning to it a dysfunctional meaning, such as the signal of underlying marital conflict. The emergence of coalitions is examined in families that have different ideologies regarding the centrality of the marital dyad and the relationship between the generations, and implications for family therapy interventions aimed at changing coalitional patterns are discussed.

Cultural conflicts within the family, or at the interface between the family and other systems, play a major role in problem formation for families that are in cultural transition or for families whose members have different racial, religious, language or ethnic backgrounds. Carlos Sluzki integrates his sensitivity to the problems of migration with an interactional view of symptoms. He presents two cases of elective mutism as examples of one of many language or learning related problems in bilingual families. The symptom is conceptualized as a mirror that reflects and reinforces, while providing a way out of double-binding circumstances linked to conflicts of loyalties between past and present, conflict between cultures, and conflict among family members.

Jan Faulkner and George Kich maintain that stereotypes about race and myths about the superiority of racial purity have contributed to a negative psychological social view of interracial marriage, and suggest that a developmental and systems framework is necessary to view the interracial couple in the therapy situation. Their paper focuses on the techniques used during initial interviews to facilitate alliance building and assessment, while being sensitive to the interracial family's social situation relative to their extended families and friendship networks; the impact of racial differences on parenting roles and styles; and identity issues for the family and the individual.

A novel angle on the matter of cultural consonance is tackled by Douglas Breunlin, Max Cornwell and Brian Cade. They focus on issues related to cultural translation of family therapy models and techniques and the accommodation that occurs between therapeutic and societal values when family therapy developed in one cultural context is applied to other cultural settings. The authors base their perspective on their personal experiences with importing and modifying structural and strategic family therapy for practice in Great Britain and Australia, and suggest guidelines to facilitate an international family therapy dialogue.

The three articles that follow offer specific tools that facilitate the observation and use of cultural dimensions in the moment-to-moment process of the family therapy session. David McGill introduces the construct of "life strategy" to refer to patterned group ethnic differences in values and ideals about family structure and development, and ways of defining and coping with life problems, that he uses as a conceptual base to organize his therapeutic approach. He describes a step-by-step cross-cultural process at each of the stages of psychotherapy, such as cultural joining, defining a problem as failure of the family's cultural life strategy, and moving the family toward new life strategies, thus activating the family's potential for a multicultural approach to problems.

A vivid and pragmatic account of a therapist's process-level attempts to become culturally attuned to families from diverse backgrounds is given by Jay Lappin. While exploring, probing and clarifying many issues family and therapist attempt to develop commonalities and convergence. A knowledge base about the culture is accompanied by an attitude that encourages the flow of new information and a challenge to fixed ideas. Thus, the cross-cultural therapist strives to achieve the most effective degree of distance from the family's culture by assuming a posture that balances the risk of cultural questioning with the respect for retaining the family's cultural integrity, much as an anthropologist joins and disengages from a culture.

John Schwartzman also borrows an anthropological lens when he proposes that learning about the family's culture from the "inside-out" is preferable to learning about culture from the "outside-in" through an a priori taxonomy. To aid this exploratory process, he designs a clinical tool based on an ethnographic model. It consists of classifying by analogy and metaphor those family behaviors and statements that indicate a world view. An ethnography also includes observation of behaviors during calendrical rites and rites of passage, and in dysfunctional families, through an understanding of the symptom as a prevented rite of passage. With the help of this ethnographic methodology the clinician "learns to learn" about the culture of each unique family.

Celia Jaes Falicov
Volume Editor
July, 1983

REFERENCES

Handel, G. *The psychosocial interior of the family.* Chicago: Aldine, 1967.

McGoldrick, M., Pearce, J., & Giordano, J. (Eds.) *Ethnicity and family therapy.* New York: Guilford Press, 1982.

ACKNOWLEDGMENT

I would like to thank Raul E. Falicov, MD, for his encouragement and helpful suggestions, and Tery Shearer for her thoughtful assistance in many tasks.

1. Normal Family Ideologies: Myths and Realities

Froma Walsh, PhD
The Family Institute of Chicago
    Center for Family Studies
Northwestern University Medical School
Chicago, Illinois

"IS OUR FAMILY NORMAL?" AS A SOCIETY, AMERICANS PLACE A GOOD deal of emphasis on being "normal" and on being "healthy." These terms, often used interchangeably, hold a variety of meanings and connotations. Further confounding the issue, our society has been changing at such an accelerated pace in recent decades that many cultural ideologies of normality have become myths, lagging behind emerging social realities and yet continuing to exert a powerful influence. The purpose of this article is to examine several cultural myths about normality that influence both the ways families regard themselves and the criteria clinicians use to assess and treat families in distress.

PERSPECTIVES ON FAMILY NORMALITY

The question "Is our family normal?" can have quite different meanings depending on one's frame of reference. In our culture, there are four major perspectives for defining normality in families: (1) asymptomatic functioning; (2) optimal functioning; (3) average functioning; and (4) transactional processes (Walsh, 1982a). Each of these perspectives on family normality has important clinical implications.

Asymptomatic Family Functioning

A family may be regarded as normal if no family member is suffering, or has a history of, symptoms of psychopathology. Normality and health are a single concept, both being equated with the absence of illness. From this perspective, a normal, healthy family is defined as one without problems displayed by any member. It is a negative definition, based on the absence of criteria of psychopathology as defined by psychiatric classifications rooted in the medical model.

Optimal Family Functioning

This perspective on normality attempts to define a normal, or healthy, family in terms of positive or ideal characteristics Optimally functioning families may be categorized at the top of a continuum, with average or asymptomatic families in the middle range, and severely dysfunctional families at the low end. The criteria for judging how healthy a family is vary depending on the values and assumptions rooted in one's world view. They

2

are oftentimes absolute judgments, based on a conviction about what is "right" or "best" for families. Most often such judgments are based on beliefs about childrearing contexts and practices that are thought to be in the best interests of child development. Only recently are empirical data being brought to bear on such judgments (Walsh, 1982b).

Average Family Functioning

From this frame of reference, a family is regarded as normal if it conforms to the average, typical, or most prevalent pattern of family life. This concept of normality, rooted in a sociological orientation, is based on statistical measures of central tendency. A family is defined as normal if it falls within the normal range; families outside that range are, by definition, abnormal. This perspective disengages the concepts of health, normality, and absence of symptoms. An optimally functioning family, at the high end of a normal distribution, is as infrequent—and thus, as deviant or abnormal—as a severely dysfunctional family. Moreover, by this definition, normal families are not necessarily asymptomatic. If most families are found to have occasional problems, the presence of a problem does not, in itself, imply that a family is not normal. This approach to defining normality is used widely to delineate expectable or predictable patterns in family interaction, such as the salient issues, tasks, and transitional processes involved at successive stages of the family life cycle.

Transactional Family Processes

From this perspective, normal families are conceptualized in terms of universal processes that are characteristic of all human systems. Basic processes involve the integration, maintenance, and growth of the family unit, in relation to both individual and social systems. What is normal— either typical or optimal—is relative to a family's social and temporal context. The criteria vary with different internal and external demands requiring adaptation over the course of the family life cycle. Judgments are largely based on how functional a pattern is, referring to the utility of a structural or behavioral pattern in achieving objectives. The judgment is contingent on the particular objectives and context: functional to what end, for whom, and in what situation. What may be functional at one systems level—individual, family, or society—may not necessarily be functional at others. A pattern that is functional at one stage of the family life cycle may be dysfunctional at another stage.

Norms as Interpersonal Rules

Any of the above perspectives on family normality may be the basis for establishing relationship norms. The sociological concept of norms refers to standards that organize and guide interaction, setting a range of conduct deemed desirable or permissible. As such, norms are interpersonal rules that proscribe and regulate behavior. Each culture has its own norms, which are established over the course of history in that society, both shaping and reflecting cultural, religious, and ethnic beliefs, assumptions, and values. Prevailing standards of what is customary, what ought to be done, and what is not tolerated are reinforced through the mores, laws, and folkways in each culture.

More precisely, social norms are people's *ideas* about what behavior is customary, right, and proper (Bott, 1971). These are views they *assume they share* with others in their society. They are not simply external standards internalized by individuals, but rather they are concepts constructed by individuals by selectively drawing on particular societal standards as they fit their experience and personal needs. Of all referents used in forming familial norms, parents provide the most important and basic models of family life, which couples attempt to emulate or improve upon. The next most important referent is the informal social network of relatives, friends, and neighbors. Third is one's own social circle and group representing a similar life style. Mass media, and television in particular, are also influential shapers and reflections of normal family images. Thus, there is a considerable range and choice in groups and categories that can be identified with, resulting in a flexibility and diversity of models of family life. At the same time, there is a tendency for people to treat their own behavior and standards, or personal views, as social norms applying to other people as well.

Concepts of family normality are used for general orientation to the social world and for evaluating one's own family and the position of others. It is important to distinguish between *ideal norms*—beliefs about optimal family functioning—and *norms of expectation*—typical patterns in average, ordinary families. Families compare themselves to both standards, just as clinicians hold views about each model. A distinction should also be made between *felt deviance* and *externally defined deviance,* a lack of correspondence, in the first case, between a family's behavior and their own social norms, and in the second case, between their behavior and the standards held by others, including clinicians. Thus, it is important for therapists to assess how a family views itself in relation to its own social norms based on its life experience and social context. Where a family sees itself as deviant—either from its view of average families in terms of norms of expectation, or from its concept of optimally functioning families in terms of ideal norms—is the perceived deviance regarded as a deficiency (something wrong with them) and is it a source of concern to them? Clinicians must not assume that a family shares their own social standards, nor that deviance (either felt deviance or externally defined deviance) is a problem requiring clinical intervention. Similarly, inconsistencies and conflicts of norms are found in all families and are not necessarily problematic for a family. Given the flexibility and variation of social norms, each family selects and interprets social norms to fit its needs and situation, and at times to justify its positions.

SOCIAL CHANGE AND DISEQUILIBRIUM

Normative standards for families can become both more important and more problematic when a society is undergoing rapid social transformation (Walsh, in press). During such a period of transition, normative conflict and confusion are likely to be heightened. As new family structures and practices have been emerging over the past two decades, traditional values and assumptions have been called into question. At the same time, relevant norms are lacking to guide families in transition as they experiment with alternative patterns of relating and adapting to a changing social world.

In a stable society, there is greater congruence between social norms pertaining to the family and actual family practices. During periods of rapid change, greater discrepancy occurs between ideology and practice as beliefs and assumptions about family life lag behind emerging social realities. When rapid change threatens the stability and continuity of traditional family patterns, many families—and sectors of the society—may resist change by rigidly adhering to traditional norms despite their questionable relevance or utility for adaptation. At such a time of disequilibrium in family and social systems, norms may be reasserted to reestablish the familiar and less threatening old order. When the discrepancies between beliefs and practices become pervasive, the norms become myths.

The concept of family myths (Ferreira, 1977) refers to well systematized beliefs and expectations shared by family members about their mutual roles and the nature of their relationships. They contain many of the covert relationship rules, the norms that govern interactional patterns within a family (Jackson, 1965). The origin of a family myth may be lost; many have been passed on for generations. Once the myth becomes operative, it may remain as an integral aspect of the relationship where it functions as an ordering force, "a buffer against sudden changes or alterations" (Ferreira, 1977, p. 53). In this sense, the family myth serves as a group defense; it promotes homeostasis and the stability of the relationship. It becomes part of the inner image of the family, expressing the way the family is seen by insiders, perceived as emotionally indispensable and an integral part of their shared reality. Myths promote ritual, provide bases for consensus, and serve as blueprints for action that require little thought or negotiation.

Myths regarding the family operate at the societal level as well and serve a similar homeostatic function for the integration and continuity of the social system. Cultural myths may be accepted unquestioningly as social norms when, in actuality, the beliefs and expectations on which they are based do not fit the experience of many, if not most, families in the society. Nevertheless, they exert a powerful influence on families' views of themselves and other families since they serve as standards for comparison and base lines for determining and judging actions. Cultural myths also have important ramifications in the clinical setting, for they influence both a family's perceptions of its own functioning and areas of dysfunction and a clinician's assessment of what is pathological. Furthermore, cultural myths influence, often covertly, the treatment goals desired by the family and objectives deemed important by the therapist. Several prevalent myths have particular relevance for family therapy and are worth examining. In each of the myths, two types of errors can be made by clinicians, who are trained to look for and treat pathology. Falicov and Karrer (1978) have defined such errors as follows. A Type I error is to mistakenly identify as pathological a pattern that is normal. A Type II error is to fail to recognize a pathological pattern in mistakenly assuming it to be normal.

CULTURAL MYTHS AND FAMILY REALITIES

Myth: Normal Families Are Problem-Free

A widely accepted belief in our society is that normal families do not have problems or conflicts. This assumption has been referred to as "the myth of placid normality" (Minuchin, 1974). This myth is actually several myths, relating to each of the perspectives on normality described above. If a family is viewed from the clinical perspective that defines normality in terms of absence of symptoms, the presence of a problem implies abnormality and family pathology. If freedom from problems is taken as a criterion for optimal family functioning, it becomes a utopian ideal that can never be reached (Watzlawick, 1977).

In reality, virtually all families have occasional problems. Stress and conflict are an expectable part of ordinary family experience, and thus problems are normal in the sense of average, predictable processes. Similarly, from a transactional systems perspective, it is erroneous to regard the normal state as homeostatic, viewing that as maintenance of a static, frictionless steady state. Rather, family systems are constantly struggling to work out a dynamic equilibrium between counterbalancing pressures for stability and change (through processes of morphostasis and morphogenesis) in confronting stressors within the family (life cycle demands) and external to the family (environmental challenges).

In regard to this myth, the Type I error is to assume that the presence of a problem in a family is necessarily a symptom of family pathology. The Type II error is to fail to note family pathology in assuming that a family presenting as problem-free is normal, as in a united front or pseudomutual family facade.

The first type of error is more common, because clinical training so heavily emphasizes the diagnosis of disorders, and when one looks carefully for something, it is more likely to be found than not. Moreover, too often clinical training fails to give sufficient attention to research and literature on normal family processes or to provide training exposure to nonclinical families. Given limited information and contact, clinicians may fail to recognize family strengths or misjudge them as dysfunctional. It is not surprising that, only half-jokingly, it has been said that ''a normal family is one that has not yet been clinically assessed.''

Families, as well, often worry that the presence of a problem means that they are not normal, that there is ''something wrong'' with them. In this author's research project, comparing families of psychiatrically hospitalized children with nonclinical families in a ''normal control group,'' recruitment of the ordinary, nonclinical families revealed two common concerns. Several families refused to participate due to concerns by some members (as reported by other members) that because they were to be interviewed in a psychiatric setting, ''problems'' might be found in their families, even though they had been informed that they were recruited as a normal control group, comprising ordinary families from all walks of life, and that their child had already been assessed as well-functioning. Even more interesting, in response to an ad in a small neighborhood paper, over 125 families volunteered, many of them (screened out) motivated to participate because they worried about whether they were normal—or disturbed—and hoped to have their normality confirmed by the researchers' findings, or more simply by being in a control group labeled as ''normal.''

Clinicians need to be more attuned to family concerns about their own normality versus abnormality when a member, or the entire family, is struggling with a problem. Much that is labeled as "resistance" in family therapy relates to family concerns that they will be judged as disturbed or the cause of a member's disturbance. Unfortunately, too many families are given the message by clinicians that they are being referred for family therapy because the problem presented by a member is "really" a family problem, that it is only a symptom of marital or family disturbance. Besides being unhelpful to a family that already worries that it has failed in some way, it is erroneous to assume that individual disorder is always a symptom of family dysfunction, or that it necessarily serves a function for the family. It is crucial to distinguish between a dysfunctional family and a normal family that is coping as well as can be expected with its problems. Furthermore, it is important to distinguish between pathology and normal, expectable problems of ordinary family life. For example, acute distress and confusing turmoil associated with a major transition in the family life cycle are quite common and should not be confused with family pathology.

Another danger in regard to this myth is to consider a problem-free state as ideal or optimal family functioning and to set unrealistic treatment goals based on the attainment of this state. Too often this leads to interminable therapy, since no matter how much progress a family makes they will always fall short of the goal as new problems inevitably arise. The quest for personal growth or family relationship enhancement may result instead in a greater sense of inadequacy and frustration in the failure to achieve the unrealistic expectations.

Myth: Normal Families Are—and Should Remain—Intact

Two myths are involved in this assumption. The first is that most families conform to the model of both biological parents remaining married and rearing their children together in one household. The second is that this model is healthier than non-intact alternatives. which are deemed harmful to children.

In reality, family structures have been changing dramatically over the past two decades in our society (Walsh, 1982a). The divorce rate has doubled since 1965. Currently one-third to one-half of all first marriages are likely to end in divorce. Consequently, almost one in five families with children is maintained by one parent in the household, usually the mother. As many as four children in ten are expected to spend at least part of their childhood in a one-parent household. Furthermore, most divorced parents remarry, creating increasing numbers of stepfamily units.

Yet, even with the recent increase in divorce, the proportion of families undergoing dissolution and remarriage is not significantly greater than in the past, when there was lower life expectancy and earlier widowhood. In fact, more children than ever before are now reared through childhood by at least one biological parent; fewer are now adopted out or institutionalized (Hareven, 1982). Thus, a sizable proportion of families in our society throughout our history has been non-intact and, therefore, must be considered part of the statistical norm, or average family experience.

The myth that intact families are inherently better environments for children is not supported by the evidence from numerous research findings. In a longitudinal study comparing a variety of family structures, no significant difference was found in impact on early childhood cognitive and socioemotional development. Among families of each form the variance was high, with some families very effective and others less so, suggesting that any of a variety of family structures holds the potential for competent parenting (Eiduson, 1979). Similarly, a recent review of research on female-headed households concluded that children were as likely to have good emotional adjustment, self-esteem, and intellectual development; and a rate of juvenile delinquency no higher than that of other children of comparable socioeconomic status (Cashion, 1982).

Therapists need to be aware of these realities so as not to make the following errors. A Type I error would be to assume that a non-intact family is inherently pathogenic. A Type II error would be to fail to note dysfunction in an intact family by assuming it is normal. Couples, in fact, often enter marital therapy with the expectation that the therapist will disapprove of divorce and "try to save the marriage." This assumption may contribute to the couple's guilt about breaking up the family and concern about the detrimental consequences for their children inherent in the breakup. Where couples are contemplating the possibility of divorce, it is most helpful for therapists to take a neutral stance, encouraging them to weigh and consider the many factors, advantages, and costs of either decision, and helping them to sort out the realities from the myths.

Myth: Healthy Families Maintain the Traditional Male/Female Role Division (Countermyth: Supermoms Do It All)

The popular image of the normal family—typical and healthy—depicts the husband/father as the sole or primary wage earner and decision maker and the wife/mother as homemaker and primary parental influence. Any deviation from this role division is regarded as pathological, both in terms of the couple's relationship and its effects on children. This widely held view has been endorsed by prominent theorists in sociology and psychiatry (Lidz, 1963; Parsons & Bales, 1955), who describe the husband's task as the family's instrumental leader and the wife's task as the socioemotional leader. Based on this model, it is assumed that there will be negative effects on children if (1) the mother is the more dominant parent, or (2) she "abdicates" her mothering role by working outside the home.

Obviously, the traditional role divisions are no longer practiced or espoused by a sizable number of families who, in increasing numbers, are attempting alternative arrangements, most often in sharing home and work roles and renegotiating the nature and rules of their relationship. Even among more traditional families, sex role relations have been changing greatly as women have assumed active roles in the work force. More than half of all mothers with school age children—and over 40% of mothers with younger children—currently work outside the home, with most in full-time jobs. This pattern reflects not only changes in women's own aspirations but also, in most cases, a growing economic necessity. Two-parent households are finding two incomes increasingly essential to maintain a moderate standard of living and to rear children through college. Also, women heading one-parent households typically are the primary or sole support of their children. In sum, the trend away from women's occupation in full-time homemaking and child care is a reality requiring changes in the functional organization of the family system and coparental unit. Moreover, research suggests that in well-functioning families it makes no significant difference which parent is the more dominant, mother or father (Lewis, Beavers, Gossett, & Phillips, 1976). Regarding the supposed detrimental effect on children of working mothers, numerous studies have found no support for this contention and some investigations have found that children in day-care services often show superior developmental abilities, particularly in cognitive and social skills.

Nevertheless, the persistence of this myth contributes to concern on the part of parents—especially working mothers—that in departing from gender norms, they will damage their children. Also, it is common for couples to experience a period of turbulence in their marital relationship when the wife's entry into the work force shifts the equilibrium and rules of the relationship from a traditional complementary role relationship to a more egalitarian symmetrical one. Issues of power, control, or a husband's feared loss of status and self-esteem may be presented clinically. Here it would be useful for therapists to explore the couple's beliefs and concerns related to cultural myths and stereotypes of normative sex roles; that is, what they, and their family and social network, regard as proper and "natural" for men and women. Second, the couple may need assistance renegotiating the terms of their relationship and the specifics of putting into practice their desire for a more egalitarian relationship and division of responsibilities in child care and homemaking. Breaking their former homeostatic pattern is often more difficult than couples expect, and may result in premature divorce when a reorganization can be achieved in therapy. Here it is crucial not to erroneously conclude—a Type I error—that the marriage is pathological or hopeless when the distress is associated with transitional difficulties.

More recently a countermyth has appeared in our society, accompanying the enormous influence of the women's movement. This is the myth of the supermom, who can—and should—"have it all," functioning to perfection as wife, mother, and career person, simultaneously juggling all responsibilities with equal expertise and remaining "problem-free." This becomes all the more problematic in cases where the husband maintains a more traditional stance or when the pressures of time and multiple demands strain the marital relationship. It would be important for a therapist to help the couple recognize that unrealistic expectations almost inevitably impose a burden on the relationship, rather than viewing the relationship as necessarily deficient, or the spouse(s) as inadequate. The problem may be in the attempt to attain a mythical ideal. It can be done by some couples, but requires enormous commitment, optimal communication, and combined structure/flexibility. Therapists can be helpful in helping couples improve these aspects of their relationship within realistic limits.

Myth: The Nuclear Family Is Isolated from Their Extended Family

According to this myth, when children in our society reach adulthood they leave home and are no longer emotionally interdependent with their families of origin. This myth has its roots in the American value of independence and in the prevalent choice of young adults to live apart from their parents, either on their own or when they marry. However, this confuses leaving home with emotional cutoff. Given this myth, perhaps it is not surprising that many families have problems at the developmental transition of launching, mistakenly assuming it will necessitate a loss of the parent-child relationship. A corollary of this myth assumes that adults are not emotionally involved with their aging parents, or consider them to be such a burden that they "dump" them in institutions (Walsh, 1980).

In reality, abundant research evidence refutes these notions. Most Americans remain emotionally attached and interdependent with their extended

families throughout adulthood (Walsh, 1980). Frequent contact and recipro-
cal support bonds are maintained despite the preference for separate households in a pattern that has been termed "intimacy at a distance." Moreover,
as adults reach midlife, they typically assume greater responsibility for
aging parents and resort to institutionalization only after exhausting all other
feasible means of caring for their elders.

In clinical practice, family relationships in the middle and later phases of
the life cycle have been neglected. Focus tends to be narrowly directed to
nuclear family relationships in early childhood and adolescence. At launching, the focus typically follows the younger generation and their families of
procreation, ignoring the three-generational, and often four-generational,
interaction that continues across the life span. Young adults tend to request,
and to be seen in, individual therapy, with attention directed to family of
origin relationships primarily or exclusively in terms of past influences from
childhood. The importance of current relations with parents tends to be
underestimated. A Type I error may be made if a therapist assumes that
emotional involvement is an indication of family pathology. Where there is
a pseudo-independent stance by distancing from threatening emotional
involvement with parents, the therapist may make a Type II error in
mistaking this reactive stance for "normal" independence when unresolved
conflict should be addressed.

Similarly, a therapist may fail to recognize the significance of recent
complications or losses in adults' relationships with their parents and siblings by erroneously assuming that they are less important than earlier
childhood influences. In particular, the impact of parent loss on adult
children as well as on their marital and family systems has been greatly
underestimated (Walsh, 1978; Walsh, 1980). In many cases, recent complications in the parent-grandparent relationship may have reverberations
throughout the three-generational family, with symptoms appearing in the
youngest generation, deflecting parental concern.

Thus, it is important for therapists to assess the three-generational family
field regardless of which generation presents symptoms, and it is imperative
to attend to the most recent interactional patterns to assess their current
impact. These relationships are all the more important in single-parent
families and in complex remarried family systems.

Myth: American Society Is a Melting Pot

This cultural myth is rooted in a patriotic allegiance to our national
identity in a society founded by and made up of immigrants. The notion of

the melting pot assumes that, through processes of acculturation, group distinctions between people of different ethnic origins dissolve as they blend in with one another in becoming Americans.

In reality, ethnicity is a powerful influence in family life and in personality development, contributing to a sense of belonging and historical continuity (McGoldrick, 1982). It patterns behavior, thinking, and feeling in both obvious and subtle ways and contributes to life choices, the celebration of holidays and rituals, and attitudes about life and death, illness and health. Language and customs influence whether or not a symptom is labeled as a problem. The experience of well-being or of being ill is strongly influenced by cultural beliefs. The conception of what is normal varies for different ethnic groups, just as family patterns differ in numerous ways. For example, some ethnic groups, such as Jewish and Italian families, value emotional expressiveness in family relationships more than others, and more than the dominant culture. Therapists need to avoid a Type I error of mistakenly diagnosing as pathology what is simply an ethnic variant from the dominant norm. Conversely, clinicians need to guard against a Type II error in failing to attend to a family problem by assuming the family fits an ethnic stereotype. Therapists, moreover, need to become more aware of their own ethnic values and beliefs and the ways they interface in their judgment of client family processes, strengths, and the definition of problems and therapeutic objectives. Problem-solving approaches and solutions should take into account and be consonant with each family's ethnic value system.

CONCLUSION

Clearly, there is no single definition or model of family normality that is representative or appropriate for all families in a society as diverse and as rapidly changing as our own. It is important for therapists to examine more carefully the normal family ideologies that clients bring with them into treatment that influence the problems they define for themselves and the solutions they seek. It may be useful to help them sort out cultural myths from realities where beliefs and expectations contribute to—or are used to justify—dysfunctional family patterns or perception of problems and health. Family therapists should also become more knowledgeable about nonclinical families to avoid biasing assessment criteria and treatment objectives with their own myths of family normality. Finally, given the diversity among normal families, it can be helpful to families in distress to normalize, where appropriate, the stresses and strains they are experiencing in their efforts to adapt in a complex social world.

REFERENCES

Bott, E. *Family and social network: Roles, norms, and external relationships in ordinary urban families* (Rev. ed.). London: Tavistock, 1971.

Cashion, B. Female-headed families: Effects on children and clinical implications. *Journal of Marital and Family Therapy*, 1982, *8*, 77-85.

Eiduson, B. Emergent families of the 1970's: Values, practices, and impact on children. In D. Reiss & H. Hoffman (Eds.), *The American family: Dying or developing*. New York: Plenum Press, 1979.

Falicov, C., & Karrer, B. *Family development and acculturation*. Paper presented at the San Francisco General Hospital Family Forum, November 1978.

Ferreira, A. Family myths. In P. Watzlawick & J. Weakland (Eds.), *The interactional view*. New York: Norton, 1977.

Hareven, T. American families in transition: Historical perspectives on change. In F. Walsh (Ed.), *Normal family processes*. New York: Guilford Press, 1982.

Jackson, D. The study of the family. *Family Process*, 1965, *4*, 1-20.

Lewis, J., Beavers, W.R., Gossett, J., & Phillips, V. *No single thread: Psychological health in family systems*. New York: Brunner/Mazel, 1976.

Lidz, T. *The family and human adaptation*. New York: International Universities Press, 1963.

McGoldrick, M. Ethnicity and family therapy: An overview. In M. McGoldrick, J. Pearce, & J. Giordano (Eds.), *Ethnicity and family therapy*. New York: Guilford Press, 1982.

Minuchin, S. *Families and family therapy*. Cambridge, Mass.: Harvard University Press, 1974.

Parsons, T., & Bales, R. *Family, socialization, and interaction processes*. Glencoe, Ill.: Free Press, 1955.

Walsh, F. Concurrent grandparent death and birth of schizophrenic offspring: An intriguing finding. *Family Process*, 1978, *17*, 457-463.

Walsh, F. The family in later life. In E. Carter & M. McGoldrick (Eds.), *The family life cycle: Framework for family therapy*. New York: Gardner Press, 1980.

Walsh, F. Conceptualizations of normal family functioning. In F. Walsh (Ed.), *Normal family processes*. New York: Guilford Press, 1982. (a)

Walsh, F. Research on normal family processes. In F. Walsh (Ed.), *Normal family processes*. New York: Guilford Press, 1982. (b)

Walsh, F. Social change, disequilibrium, and adaptation in developing societies, In J. Schwartzman (Ed.), *Macrosystemic approaches to family therapy*. New York: Guilford Press, in press.

Watzlawick, P. The Utopia syndrome, In P. Watzlawick & J. Weakland (Eds.), *The interactional view*. New York: Norton, 1977.

2. A Perspective for the Use of the Cultural Dimension in Family Therapy

Braulio Montalvo, MA
Philadelphia Child Guidance Clinic
and
Bryn Mawr College
Graduate School of Social Work and Social Research
Philadelphia, Pennsylvania

Manuel Gutierrez, PhD
Aspira, Inc.
Philadelphia, Pennsylvania

The authors have worked, directly and through supervision and consultation, with a variety of ethnic families. For the past 3 years they have collaborated on a longitudinal research study on Puerto Rican youths in Philadelphia.

The authors wish to thank Nell Anderson and Marcia Vitiello for their comments and suggestions, and Dr. Pedro Herscovici, Jay Lappin, Edwin Roldan, and Sam Scott for sharing their inventive work with the reality behind the masks. For the concept of therapeutic solvents we are indebted to Dr. R.R. Pottash.

CULTURE: REALITY BEHIND MASKS

To be fortunate in dealing with the cultural dimension in family therapy is to be ignorant enough to discover the family's basic problem-solving characteristics rather than its cultural baggage. The family can offer the therapist a cultural mask, a profile of who they presumably are, rather than show the essential ways in which they tend to operate when attempting to resolve their dilemmas. By flashing masks, families can confuse any therapist. For example, youngsters in a Vietnamese family can abandon their cultural mandate to be good sons (Lappin & Scott, 1982). They can show lack of consideration for the illiterate mother by insisting on using English (the language of the host culture) at home. By leaving mother out, they undermine her position. And they can do all this claiming that they are at the mercy of a cultural gap: "It's just easier to talk English here." The mother, contrary to the position her own cultural legacy endorses, stops fighting for her rights and for means to restore her dignity. She may even help to disqualify herself further because "our way" calls for "sacrifice" rather than interference with the boys' adjustment. An Italian family can justify its hovering intrusiveness around a daughter who courts a boyfriend on the porch, stating "This is our way of being; we are always together." Or they can claim, "Look, we come from Palermo where the woman does not leave the house until she is much older, until she can find her own housing." By using cultural constraints selectively, by employing references to realistic socioeconomic pressures, and by parodying ethnic blueprints, the family can pull the therapist away from reality. The therapist is made to deal instead with a cultural image of the ethnic group. In this process the family—as simply people having difficulties in solving problems—is lost.

From the standpoint taken in this article, there is no guarantee that "knowledge of the culture" permits the therapist to become necessarily more effective in dealing with families. Therapists can be creatively assimilated by families. By manipulating and restricting the therapist's attention to shared aspects of their way of being, families use culture as a defense. Therapists do well not to know too much and, instead, to let the family guide them through the idiosyncratic aspects of the culture, keeping all the while a watchful eye on broader invariants such as the process of subcultural confinement. That process entails those relationships between the minority subculture and the host culture which tend to have as an outcome the curtailment of exploration and adjustment in members of the subculture. By focusing on broader processes connecting the minority culture to its immediate surroundings, therapists prevent themselves from being distracted by specific features that make a culture distinctive. Since the effects of prolonged socioeconomic obstacles are almost routinely confused with cultural factors, this anchorage point is necessary for disentangling what is due to cultural legacy from what is due to being poor.

Of course, the appreciation of the cultural dimension matures if the therapist has dealt with families from different ethnic backgrounds and socioeconomic status. For example, with Middle Eastern families the therapist may discover that long-held sexist patterns of women's subordination cannot be undone simply by an upward change in the family's position on the socioeconomic ladder. The appreciation also sharpens if the therapist has experienced the opposite: families brought up with presumably rigid culturally sponsored patterns of sexist subordination who changed as they shifted their place in the stratification framework.

In dealing with the possibility of being distracted by cultural masks, it helps if therapists orient themselves beyond the elements making this family a member of a particular ethnic group. This means searching for what is basic to families rather than what are idiosyncratic cultural dimensions that tend to make the family alien to the therapist. The focus is on the fundamental cross-cultural requirements of being a family such as the maintenance of marriages or the fundamentals of socializing children. The therapist's goal must be a generalized flexibility rather than specialized sensitivities toward a particular ethnic group. With such an orientation, therapists can determine the limits of what they would feel at home with, and those limits come to depend more on the nature of the problem and their competence in dealing with it than on the relationship style or the cultural or ethnic background of the family.

Culture becomes a troublesome dimension in family therapy when the therapist stops wondering if he* is attributing psychopathology to a person who is really behaving normally as defined by that person's particular culture. The therapist may have feared mistaking as pathological, for instance, the seeing of a vision which, when explored in the family and its ethnic group, turns out not to be so. This healthy fear of misjudging, still alive among beginning clinicians, motivates therapists to learn how to determine, with the help of the family, if a hallucinatory experience is or is not handicapping to the participant's existence and how it functions in

---

*Aspen editors and authors are instructed to follow the Guidelines for Nonsexist Language of the American Psychological Association in preparing manuscripts for publication. Occasionally, in singular constructions that do not lend themselves to rewriting, the masculine pronoun may be used in its traditional genderless sense if such usage will result in improved clarity of expression.

holding the family together. In the process, therapists find out what in the family is fairly independent of culture. Except for certain conditions in which cultural environments press too severely upon the requirements for survival as a family, the limits of those requirements seem rather broad. Enormous variations in family customs and beliefs can be handled by therapists without becoming alien, unhelpful, and in need of special training in cultural backgrounds. This is because in all cultures the family has to protect youngsters, offering biological and psychological security while preparing them for the society in which they are to live. And in most cultures this seems to be done by adults who are simultaneously working to maintain some kind of stability for their own marital arrangement. The therapist can bypass the observed complexity and center instead on the family's underlying simplicity. With a few concepts such as conflict and collaboration, contradiction and clarity, hierarchical and nonhierarchical relationships, and flexibility and rigidity, the field of patterns of relationships narrows itself. The search for predictable sequences cuts across ethnic variations to reveal information on organization, stability, hierarchy, and continuity in all families. We search in all of them for information on the way in which a dialogue has outcome: in terms of congruent or incongruent positions, superiority or inferiority, and competency or frustration during or after conflict.

To cultivate a cultural outlook that cuts across ethnic variations, the therapist must beware of common pitfalls. It is possible to become merely delighted and empathic toward the exotic aspects of the family's culture rather than focused on how these are employed to facilitate or block problem solving. To refrain from being merely delighted or empathic, the therapist must be concerned with more than just seeing the culture from within. The therapist observing the family from within the culture may perceive the family's boundaries as less wired or more wired to the outside than they really are. To achieve a clearer picture, the therapist needs to work as well from the outside, with a skeptical, cross-cultural and interinstitutional perspective. In stories describing human problems such as alcoholism, paraphrenia, delirium, and dementia, a recent study (Benus, 1982) searched for patterns of institutional utilization among older Puerto Ricans and Ukrainians in Philadelphia. It found that Puerto Ricans were less likely than older Ukrainians to recognize that alcoholism was a problem. Alcoholism eats away unmercifully at Puerto Rican families, destroying emotional and physical health. Yet the magnitude of the problem, looking from within the culture, is not seen. The culture fails to mobilize its institutions to deal with it. For the family therapist, the concern with the family's use of institutions is helpful in breaking away from the intrafamilial event. It is important in finding the link to outside problems that may be shared by other minority cultures.

Consider the plight of the dropout minority youngster in the process of looking for employment. To deal with this situation, the therapist must see what takes place between the family and the outside world of jobs. The therapist must be aware that the father's relationship to the world of occupations tends to be a decisive force in what is going to happen to that youngster in his own first job. This tendency is certainly confirmed among Philadelphia's Puerto Rican dropouts (Gutierrez & Montalvo, 1980). Contrary to expectations, most youngsters in this group do not come from a single-parent family, but from a two-parent family with a father who has no job. The approach to fathers and sons then cannot be strictly in terms of their function in the intricate triangle with mother, but on how those triangular relationships preclude or facilitate the youngster's coping with a predictably troublesome transition to a narrowing job market. To work with this focus is realistic and economical, because what is involved is not only the youngster's personal adjustment, but the whole family's adjustment to a stratification ladder where mobility and mental health are sacrificed.

AN INTERINSTITUTIONAL PERSPECTIVE

The interactions between the family and the occupational institutions are harder to spot when families operate with a slowly unfolding script. When the unit of observation expands into the future, what is presumably a problem in these family dramas often turns out to be adaptive behavior. For instance, a young woman's puzzling retreat from college is difficult to understand. She had good grades and a fair social life, so neither therapist nor family can figure out her behavior. Much later, it becomes clear that her boyfriend is unable to succeed in an academic career and is soon to disappear into the factory world. The young woman's problem was only a stage in organizing her future status. As a college woman she would not fit with a man lacking a college education. But more than love of boyfriend pulled her back. Whether she was pulled back by a fierce class belongingness that demands a return to her socioeconomic strata, or by a patriarchal blueprint dictating that as a woman she would never be superior to the man—or by both—it behooves the family therapist to sense the compelling power of the long-range sociocultural scripts. Those scripts reveal the family's deep interconnections with the industrial context and the need for an interinstitutional perspective.

Western culture has organized the family to serve the industrial context instead of the reverse, so that a person's self-esteem and organization of the future are intimately bound up with the opportunities and tribulations of the occupational world. Therapists who work with this issue, particularly those dealing with jobless families among low socioeconomic cultural minorities, learn to revert with the family to a preindustrial model of family functioning. There is, however, one important difference. The family of the 1980s no longer has the option of packing bag and baggage and moving in the hope of finding work elsewhere. The family could wind up not only with no job but with no friends. The issue for therapists then is to help the family to stay put, if necessary, as they search for new ways of earning a living. They support the man's productiveness around the house and help segregate self-esteem from the outside job. They align themselves with the man toward an adaptive, detached, working-class attitude that "a job is just a job." They rescue whatever the man can learn in the world of layoffs about how to save pride while honestly putting out "looking for a job" efforts. They fight beliefs that hamper adaptation to reality, like the belief of many workers that their economic future is "in their hands." In fact, it is outside their direct influence (Inkeles, 1979). This belief amounts to a serious and widespread culturally patterned defect (Fromm, 1956), capturing many a man who consumes himself in tension over a job he cannot get, insisting it is his fault and feeling that he is in charge of an occupational fate far beyond his control. To the extent that such a man also convinces his family of this belief, he leaves himself no supportive resources.

To help these families assess their own cultural baggage and disengage from unhelpful ideas, the therapist assists the natural process of keeping the faith, learning to wait, distorting time, making a lot of time feel like less, and orienting the self to take refuge in the simple heroics of everyday life. The effort is toward survivorship, and toward getting rid of the belief that it is all up to them. This is done, whenever possible, by assisting without making explicit the process of assistance. Two brief examples partially illustrate these notions and suggest values that can organize an interinstitutional perspective.

Watching a very poor Puerto Rican family through a one-way mirror, one sees a mother, a father, two small children, and a 10-year-old boy who looks very agitated. The boy is on his own, somewhat poorly supervised, while the mother and father and a very quiet 4-year-old daughter hover busily around a whining infant. It is obvious that the one they cannot focus on is the 10-year-old, who is getting the family into immediate trouble with the authorities because he sets fires in the basement of their apartment building. Observing this session, one is struck by the therapist's apparent lack of compassion toward this mother and father who are overburdened with a sickly infant. The therapist asks unemotionally where father works, if mother has a relative she can call to come in and help, and how often she prepares bottles for the baby. The mother, in a tone as flat as that of the therapist, seldom looks up while mumbling, "I have nothing to call with"; "Give me a pin"; "Let me have the bottle." Throughout all of this, mother keeps ministering to the baby while presumably not listening too intently. The therapist's questions bounce about like disconnected intrusions upon people busy with essential needs. Finally the therapist blurts out, "Do you think a phone would be a good idea?" Mother simply continues her activities, and father keeps fussing with the bottle and the diaper bag. The therapist was already standing up and helping the family leave the room when he said to himself, "Maybe by the time the phone shows up next week, those trips to the basement may be changing." To the very end, the interaction was rough and disjointed. Yet by the following week, the boy's fire-setting had dramatically diminished. Both the therapist and the family had carefully avoided showing themselves as people searching for favors. No open assertion of needs and no possibilities of humiliation ever surfaced. The giving, like the asking, avoided acts of generosity, helping without overexposing necessity. As the therapist assisted with obtaining a phone for "pediatric trouble," the mother and father assisted by taking charge of the older boy. The interclass and intercultural communication had been effective because the therapist and the family had traded "on the side" without obligations.

In another instance, a therapist worked with a mother, a father, and a young child in a Puerto Rican family where the boy's constant crying and inability to sleep had become the presenting problem. The father was unskilled, unable to speak English, and trying repeatedly to enter a very limited job market. In the process of constant defeats, he was becoming extremely depressed and schizoid. He hung around the apartment in a daze. At some point, he started becoming increasingly busy with the boy, until he felt that his essential role in life was to take care of him. In the meantime, his wife was growing fearful that her husband would lose control and attack the child. She had observed that many times he had been on the verge of hurting him. She saw her husband glued to her child, but unable to accept the child's constant demands without exploding. The resolution of this case began with the family acknowledging, with the help of the therapist, that their son was becoming not only a very difficult job, but *the* job. From there, it became possible to release the father by conveying to the mother and to him that he should be out of the apartment even if he could not get an outside job. The prevention of child abuse and the lifting of this man's depression hinged on dealing with two converging forces holding him hostage: first, the wife, who was holding him because of her own overt fears of being alone in the apartment; and second, the man's own working-class conscience which, like his fearful wife, would not let him leave to have some leisure: "You have no right to fun unless you are working."

Husband and wife were helped to agree that he could be out playing billiards or dominos with friends, as long as he also looked for a job. The wife joined her husband and the therapist in externalizing some of the responsibility for not finding a job. They did not take it all within the family. As the man drew once more upon his culture for the right to fun—that festive attitude that permits a Puerto Rican male to feel entitled to pleasure regardless of whether times are good or bad—the woman's fear that her husband would abuse the child was assuaged.

The young son, who had changed his cycle to napping briefly during the day and then becoming active at night to play with father, no longer was needed to protect his father from coming in contact with feelings of defeat. He immediately became accessible to the mother, who took over and organized him into more appropriate patterns of eating and sleeping.

The therapist's efforts to maintain the man's changed behavior continued: "You have to keep yourself in a fairly good mood to continue looking for a job." Those efforts brought out the wife's covert fear that the man would, as in years past, allow himself to be swallowed up by billiards and dominos. He might even slip forever into the world of alcohol. That fear was contained by constantly anticipating it. It was emphasized that he had to get out of the house anyway, if his son was to become healthy, and his wife was to learn how to manage herself and the apartment without fear of being alone.

Both of these instances entail approaches to the cultural dimension which require no specialized training but do reflect certain priorities. The first is mindful of the possibility of subordination and humiliation inherent in working with poor families. The second disconnects self-esteem from the depriving and oppressive occupational reality of a postindustrial society. Not all men in such a society can compensate inside the family for what happens outside. This is true particularly when the outside threatens with permanent structural unemployment. Some, as in our illustration, compound their pathology and that of their immediate family when attempting to do so, because their effort is at odds with their traditional family format. In that format a woman's competence and status remain closely hinged to her performance as mother and housekeeper inside the home, and a man's competence and esteem remain closely linked to his wage-earner role outside the home. Results from our recent survey of dropouts provide evidence that deviations from that design shape a difficult transition. While 48% of the mothers of dropouts had a marital relationship, only 22% indicated that there was another adult in the house who helped with the children. Since most fathers of dropouts were unemployed *and* at home, it was clear that few men were experienced as supportive in terms of helping out with parenting tasks. These men were either functioning as usual in the family, remaining basically uninvolved, or if trying to be helpful were not perceived as such.

TACTICAL USE OF CULTURE

Perhaps the best approach to the cultural dimension derives from self-propelled therapists who organize themselves around their ignorance of the family's culture. They search for the family's ways of thinking by having the family teach them the ways of the culture, making a tactical advantage out of the difference in cultures. These therapists ask to be guided as to the meaning of certain customs, practices, mores, or language. For example, the therapist can have the family teach him the key insults in the culture. By learning the most powerful words, the charged meanings in the culture, the therapist equips himself to characterize behavior and to alter interpersonal patterns of subordination, enslavement, and enmeshment which work against family members. These patterns call for strong solvents, words of great affective power, that can be instrumental in shaking up people and starting change. There is no more effective way of confronting a Puerto Rican man who ignores that rare, better job chance, and who is too accepting of a job where he is exploited, than through well-timed use of choice insults in his culture. At the appropriate moment, and with the right intensity, the therapist can wonder out loud whether someone this man values thinks he is a "pendejo" (sucker) or a "jibaro" (peasant), with his boss, or with peers in the job. "Does your wife think they see you as a 'jibaro' over there?" In a context of mutual integrity, these interventions can do much to start the process of eroding particular patterns. Of course, if misused, or used like quick recipes, without trust and earned consent, the insult will backfire and jeopardize the therapy. Generally, however, even the most frontal insults are well tolerated when coming from somebody with a strange accent and who is unquestionably respectful.

For all these approaches, the therapist needs access to the private world of images of the culture. That world is never so private as to conceal the powerful impact of a sustained, oppressive socioeconomic outside. A sub-sample of respondents in our study answered the question "What do you want for the youngster's future?" with raw survival values and realistic fears: "I hope he doesn't get beat up on the way to school"; "I hope my daughter does not become a whore"; "I hope my son does not die from drugs," and so forth. For these families, stress and danger constitute a constant—the rule during inevitable life transitions. The shift from home to school brings the fear-based problems: shyness, phobias, and mutism. The shift from school to work brings with it the possibilities of chronic addiction and crime. During both of these shifts, the cultural dimension becomes part of a profile that can be confusing to helping institutions and clinicians.

CONFUSING PROFILES

From Home to School

Among the diverse problems affecting Hispanic children during the transition from home to school, elective mutism seems to be increasing in recent years. In our observations, these children tend to come from two-parent families: very much home centered, usually religious, and traditional. A salient characteristic is that most of these families do not have much social interaction with the outside world. There is more than a nuance of fear of the outside world. With it comes a lot of caution that is communicated to the children about how to deal with what is out there. The home life may be rich, but the life outside the family is notably limited. In general, the parents in these families are often quite noncommunicative with English-speakers although they can easily hold a conversation with a Spanish-speaking person. There is an obvious concern with language and the difficulties it presents, and a discomfort about communicating in English. This is hard to separate from a generalized caution toward the outside world. Along with the parental characteristics, we see in the youngsters a history of unfortunate incidents in the first contacts with the outside. They have usually been frightened by an outsider. In many cases, the first contact with the outsider turns out to be a troublesome contact with a scary figure and soon, following that incident, comes the first contact with the preschool. That one, too, turns out to be unfortunate, frightening the child even further.

Yet among the requirements for shaping an elective mute, we seldom see the teacher directly traumatizing the child. More frequently, the school environment—during recess, in the yard, or in the classroom—may have allowed the child to witness another child, a peer, being abruptly treated by an intimidating adult. Perhaps a child was being reprimanded for stepping out of line or talking too much. The most pathetic of arrangements are those in which the school also intimidates, wittingly or unwittingly, the parents.

They visit the school and come to see the personnel there as experts who control the situation and are going to fix the problem. The parents may have questions, but they hesitate to ask them.

Previous theory has failed to give sufficient weight to the school as a fear-inducing institution. It has been easier to put emphasis on shifting the child's internal dynamics in order for the youngster to talk. It was thought that by getting the youngster's dynamics to change, the youngster would talk, first in the extended family (among relatives) and then in school. The family and the school were simply secondary scenes where symptoms were displayed.

That viewpoint was abandoned as the field of therapy went on to consider the obvious cultural and linguistic differences as the main issue. Since the cultural clash had chosen language as its battleground, it became important for the school to work with the parents to make the youngster comfortable around language, so that the child could absorb whatever the school could provide. This viewpoint recognized the ground between the school and the family as an arena for a tug of war, and for disdain, prejudice, and other judgmental attitudes that could be deleterious to the resolution of the problem. However, with this approach the child often felt that his parents went along with the adults in the school. Sometimes the child would feel that he had lost his fundamental allies to the school authorities. If a therapist was involved, he worked with a "child guidance" model with the child's play and fantasy. Only incidentally were the parents touched, and seldom the school. Now that, too, has changed; and there are new problems for the therapist. These come with the possibility of too much active intervention with the school, in which the therapist lives out a rescue fantasy that does not allow the parents to become competent.

The problem of elective mutism confuses the mental health settings and the school, because there is always enough interesting material pointing to the "cause" of the problem in the family. Usually there are parents who are shy, who do not talk much, who show some generalized avoidance of the outside. It becomes easy for the school not to look carefully at what it contributes to the problem. The school's classic way of perpetuating the problem is to operate from a time oriented perspective. "Let's just give her more time," or "Let's give the culture more time to assimilate, time for the child to feel more comfortable." When the family finally makes a move and goes to the school, the child is completely entrenched in a nonparticipating status.

The school often operates on the assumption (explicit or not) that the foreign culture needs time to integrate itself into the host culture. The school does not need to reach out to the child; it is the child who must reach out to the school. Let the subculture accommodate to the host culture. The school tends to rationalize its activity through a developmental perspective: we are waiting for the child's readiness.

Generally, parents are kept subordinate and expectant, made to rely on the "expert" adults in the school who will repair the problem in the child. But the unstimulating situation generated in the school cannot unfreeze the child from his special status as nonparticipant, and the family is called in to deal with the situation. The school then proceeds either by doing too much or too little. In almost all cases of Hispanic elective mutism we have had to actively reengage the parents with the school personnel, strongly supporting the parents to exert initiative and authority over the manner in which the child is being handled. More often than not, the parents start requesting from the school that more be expected of the child; and the child changes. When the interinstitutional situation is reversed—and the school makes requests on the parents, who start in turn to make requests on the child—problems are compounded. The situation seems to be more amenable to change when there is an imbalance, when the parents are established clearly as allies of the child, rather than of the school. Expectations of balanced collaborations between school and family, desirable for other purposes, do not seem appropriate for purposes of problem solving.

A most promising approach seems to focus on a remedy for the discomfort and lack of assertiveness the parents feel in coping not just with the child but with the outside in general. In this case, the outside is not just the school. They must deal with the demands of shopping, taking public transportation, and so forth. As parental confidence and competence develop in these other areas, changes in their expectations of the school occur; and changes for the child become possible.

The problem of elective mutism is most likely to occur among recent arrivals and in children of spouses who have been here for a while but remain monolingual (Spanish only). The elective mute enacts the subculture's efforts at pacing, at resisting change and modulating the rate of assimilation into the host culture. The elective mute is organized around issues of intimidation and lack of confidence in dealing with the new outside culture. These issues are likely to have been already negotiated by the more acculturated second generation families. What is most evident in second generation families is their involvement, not in resisting or regulating change, but in facilitating quick change. They serve as a mechanism for fast modification of language and culture. They may even lose it altogether. In a recent study of second generation families (Gutierrez & Montalvo, 1982), about 62% spoke both languages; about 66% were married within their own ethnic group; and 35% were using "English only" when dealing with their spouses. That 35% were couples mediating the loss of language for the next generation. They used Spanish as an intergenerational link, in talking with their own parents, but were unlikely to employ it with their children to ensure cultural transmission.

From School to Work

The transition from school to work brings special dilemmas to the family from a minority culture. Consider the Puerto Rican family in the United States. As the youngster makes this transition, the family reassesses the larger culture. They look again at the dream of a better life here for the second generation, and they take stock of whether they have realized it or not. Thoughts reemerge of possible return to the island, of bridges burned, and of the possibility that it is too late. For many, the reappraisal brings the pain of knowing that the family will not make it. If there is nothing for the son, then the possible demoralization of the family and the abdication of the adults are at stake. And all this happens when the danger of the family's breakdown of discipline and vigilance or supervision is at its peak. The youngsters are bigger, and they are rooted more outside than inside the family. They are more dependent on the peer world, thus severely testing the family's capacity to transmit positive values. The young man is out of physical jurisdiction, roaming, testing the outside world. Family resources for respecting and controlling at a distance are challenged, since the direct physical means that may have worked previously can no longer be employed. Yet this is precisely the time when the context of drugs and crime pulls the hardest, stressing the whole fabric of the culture and the family. From within the family comes the wish for the outside to offer some possibility of hope and stability. It wants jobs that are acceptable, and an environment that is not totally incongruent, oppressive, and defeating. At this stage, once again, the process of subcultural confinement exerts its power. Through a variety of setbacks, the youngster and the family find themselves unable to master the tasks that could lead to successful adjustment in this culture.

The impact of failure for such a youngster in his first attempts to get a job is greater if he is the son of a father who has been in and out of the job market. The same is true for a youngster whose father proves to be chronically unemployed. In this dilemma, the Puerto Rican youngster just joins the minority youngster from other subcultures. Both live with certain socioeconomic obstacles simply because of minority membership.

Among youngsters who have not dropped out, who got their diplomas, many go on to try the world of work and to discover painfully that their schooling has left them unequipped. Inadequate schools homogenize the youngsters as a group, leaving them without the tools necessary to master the points of entry into the host culture's job market. And if they do enter the market, the criticism of competing workers—and their own view of their performance—make it obvious that they have no basic skills. Without enough language or arithmetic to negotiate with peers and superiors on the job, they experience defeat after defeat, increasing the opportunities for sliding into delinquent experimentation. As employability becomes increasingly remote, their sense of personal worth becomes endangered. For some youngsters this danger is everything. It influences them to the point of ceasing to look for work. Stopping becomes a way of avoiding a total devaluation of self and demoralization of the family. These youngsters think it is easier to have the family think "he just doesn't look hard enough for a job" than for them to think "there is nothing for him."

For families where father has been chronically out of work, unique psychological dangers exist. The family may have been harboring some silent hope based on the youngster's chances for the future. As a family, they may have been resigned to the fact that father would never have a job. But they were saving some pride, expecting the son eventually to get a job. When the son does not, the proverbial last straw is reached and the experiment of coming to the United States in search of a better life blows up in their faces. Many families at this point surrender to chaos, guilt, and depression, increasing the possibility of drugs and alcohol experimentation. With that experimentation comes further entrenchment into the world of the unemployable, ruining the motivation to go to work and the ability to stick with the job. Drug use that began simply as a temporary tensional outlet tends to capture the participants as they come up against the limited opportunities of the outside market.

A confusing development occurs for youngsters whose fathers have become figureheads. These men have retained powers of ultimate sanction, but they participate less and less in the socialization of the youngsters or in decisions for running the household. For these families, the necessity to maintain the appearance that the father has not lost all authority is magnified. It is clear to the youngsters that father has no guidance to offer, particularly in terms of the job market. Father has no network of friends with jobs. He is not like fathers in families of Italian, Irish, or German extraction. They have been able to evolve traditional threads to certain trades, to unions through which they can ease the problem of access to jobs for their sons. The

Philadelphia-Puerto Rican youngster who looks to his father finds no such legacy. He sees only a world of peers on which he must rely. As that world of peers increases its pull, that of father keeps decreasing. The need to maintain some semblance of power for the father intensifies, and this is clear in the talk about him during family sessions. He is portrayed in domineering terms. Some families present a gap between what he is and what is said about him. The more the family members talk about his tyrannical strictness, the more ineffectual he becomes. In other families the father conforms to this image. He is, indeed, overbearing and bossy, particularly in his control of females. He makes up for eroded authority by holding down the women. He makes sure they remain chained to traditional in-the-home jobs.

To the Anglo therapist outside the Puerto Rican culture, these families come across as rigid patriarchal cartoons, victims of a feudal historical legacy. The contemporary issue is usually missed: the more the man fails against competitive barriers of the American society, the more uncompromising and absolute his power must be at home. The loss of the man's mastery over the culture at large is compensated for within the family. Mother, particularly, does most talking in agencies. In explaining an addiction, she points first to father's despotic negligence or strictness to account for the son's rebellion. This assigns the father powerful, though negative, responsibility and authority. This presentation often confuses the family diagnosis. The family's most impressive problem at this stage, with youngsters from 16 into the 20s, is not an excess of authority but rather the opposite. It has difficulty exerting self-respecting authority so as to prepare the youngsters to leave the family (Haley, 1980). When the youngster flirts with drugs and alcohol, the parents have trouble mobilizing their assertiveness to get him to stop or to reroute his efforts to the outside world; to looking for jobs, or keeping a job. Most often the family tries, but cannot muster enough indignation or constructive anger. It provides, instead, a sheltering response, a forgiving stance toward the youngster's experimentation with drugs.

When the family works at optimal capacity, the parents dare to be firm and risk the possibility of disunity and dismemberment. For too many families of addicts who enter therapy, this is a difficult, unnatural, almost immoral, move. It goes against the value that their particular culture places on family togetherness and unity. Attempts to hold someone accountable, responsible, to remove roof or shelter because he is not living within the rules of the family—these are painful tactics to deploy and maintain. It is almost impossible to render family membership conditional to a son or husband, even when he threatens to destroy the family through expensive drug habits and bizarre or violent conduct. Counting on that (Puerto Rican, Italian, Black, etc.) compassion, to which he feels he has unconditional access, the addict can drag down a whole family. If he can show his need for the family, expressing some guilt and some wish to be with them, the family—in most cultures—tends to reaccept him without the necessity of behavioral change.

The difficulty for the Puerto Rican family at this stage is that it exercises almost no measure of control over the addiction, which is viewed as the force of destiny. The addicted family member would rather confess that he is worthless, and a source of shame and dishonor to the family, than work to rid himself of drugs. Those families who dare leave the addicts outside, force them to grasp at other institutions involved with control over sinfulness and destiny. They grab on to Alcoholics Anonymous, or the Pentecostal churches, and by means of a dramatic conversion process rescue themselves from the formidable forces of alcohol and drugs, reentering at once both the family and the mainstream of addicts who have "cured themselves."

If the common denominator in families of chronic addicts is a manner of coping with a rule-breaking member rather than a particular ethnic or cultural background, one would never know from therapists' comments. For the therapists who come from the particular cultural background of the addict, working with these family patterns can be delusional. They come to think the cultural dimension is all. The therapist is sure that his culture is especially hard to change and that other cultures get out of the addiction rut more easily: "No one can be so forgiving as our Puerto Ricans"; "No one can put up with so much as the Irish"; "Only Italian blood ties can take this," and so forth. Therapists from all cultures, it seems, blame the indulgent, nurturing forces. The unconditional sheltering response is seen as the obstacle to rehabilitation and the main determinant of chronic addictive behavior.

CONCLUSION

Families can use the cultural dimension as a mask, as justification for curtailing needed problem solving. But the intrusive family from Palermo can also drop its mask, and its members can find a way of politely excusing themselves, disappearing to the back of the house or to the second floor to allow their daughter privacy with her boyfriend. That alternative was as available in their cultural tradition as their previous intrusiveness. Similarly, the Vietnamese youngsters, with the help of a family therapist, can agree to speak only Vietnamese at home, slowing down the generational rift until mother can master some words in English and establish new means of bonding between the youngsters and herself. In the process, she recovers her executive position, which is as compatible with her cultural tradition as the earlier need to "sacrifice" for her youngsters.

Since families can use their cultural repertoire and uniqueness to hide their basic patterns of functioning, a focus on interinstitutional dilemmas seems more useful for family therapists than a focus on cultural uniqueness. This does not deny the importance of cultural uniqueness. Puerto Rican families in Philadelphia are not so fundamentally changed by their experience in the United States that they cannot be recognized by Puerto Ricans in New York or Puerto Rico. Enough continuity of unchangeable habits, customs, manners, and ways of interpreting the world occurs to allow families, despite adjustment to local conditions, to remain recognizably Puerto Rican. But to appreciate this core of uniqueness does not require specialized training in the group's cultural and social traditions. The therapist can discover those cultural traditions when fresh contrast abounds as the family unit shapes itself with the therapist as a participant. When a family comes in contact with a therapist, its members arrange themselves so as to guard against the outsider before he can impose the outside on them. By capitalizing on being the outsider, the therapist allows the family to bring to bear its cultural legacy in spontaneous ways. Those ways will be evident in the family's reactions in the immediacy of the sessions. They will also be displayed around the inevitable shifts from one institutional sector to another—from home to school, or from school to work. Since these transitions are marked by invariant, preorganized problems, an interinstitutional perspective seems essential for coping with them.

The overwhelming fact of exchange—of interaction between the family of the subculture with the institutions of the host culture—has to be central to any understanding of the cultural dimension in family therapy. To make the cultural dimension more central than the family's interactions with the surrounding institutions is to invite excesses, both emotional and technical. Emotionally, therapists will feel that unless they are within the skin of the culture, they understand little and can do less. Technically, therapists will require training in each particular ethnic and cultural background, confusing credentials on ethnicity with problem-solving skills. The result would be a set of overspecialized, baroque therapies in a field that still lacks basic research on methods as well as outcome.

REFERENCES

Benus, H. *The impact of ethnicity on seeking assistance for mental health problems.* Unpublished doctoral dissertation, University of Maryland, 1982.

Fromm, E. Individual and social origins of neuroses in personality. In C. Kluckholm, H. Murray, & D. Schneider (Eds.), *Nature, society and culture*. New York: Alfred H. Knopf, 1956.

Gutierrez, M., & Montalvo, B. *Choice of non-delinquent and delinquent careers among Puerto Rican dropouts*. Interim Report #1. Project funded by the National Institute of Juvenile Justice and Delinquency Prevention, 1980.

Gutierrez, M., & Montalvo, B. *Aspirantes in Philadelphia*. Project funded by the Tinker Foundation, 1982.

Haley, J. *Leaving home*. New York: McGraw Hill, 1980.

Inkeles, A. Continuity and change in the American national character. In S.M. Lipsett (Ed.), *The third century: America as a post-industrial society*. Stanford, Calif.: Hoover Institutions Press, 1979.

Lappin, J., & Scott, A. Intervention in a Vietnamese refugee family. In M. McGoldrick, J. Pearce, & J. Giordano (Eds.), *Ethnicity and family therapy*. New York: Guilford Press, 1982.

3. Culture and Class in the Study of Families

Guillermo Bernal, PhD
University of California
San Francisco, California

Ana Isabel Alvarez, PhD
City College of San Francisco
San Francisco, California

THIS ARTICLE WILL PRESENT A MODEL FOR THE INTEGRATION OF CULTURE and class in the study of families. The model grew out of extensive clinical experience with families with diverse ethnic, socioeconomic, historical, and political backgrounds. Further, the model developed from struggle and contradictions that surfaced at family study groups, family therapy seminars, and discussions with colleagues and students. While still in a formative preliminary stage, it may facilitate and refine the understanding of families across cultures and, in particular, of Hispanic families. An appreciation and critical understanding of cultural and socioeconomic history are essential for effective clinical work. Additionally, the model may serve as a framework for clinicians and researchers who wish to step out of their context in order to more accurately assess family processes.

CULTURAL AND ECONOMIC DIMENSIONS IN FAMILY STRUCTURE

The need to develop parameters for the assessment of families that are applicable cross-culturally and valid within the culture serves as our point of departure. The position taken here is that family structure and function are largely determined by economic and cultural factors. As a social structure, the family interacts with other structures of society. It is essential to take into account the transactions of the family with other structures of society to understand the nature of the family. Clearly, a study of the family is a micro study of the culture in which it is embedded.

Culture can be defined as "socially transmitted or learned ideas, attitudes, traits of overt behavior and suprapersonal institutions" (Steward, 1972). The concept of culture and its concomitant methodologies developed from a study of tribes, which are typically small, self-contained, and culturally homogeneous. Contemporary modern nations are more complex sociocultural systems that require additional dimensions of analysis.

If culture is one dimension that conditions family life, then a study of cultural values would yield important information about family processes. One of the pioneers developing a research framework for analyzing cultural values was Florence Kluckhohn (Kluckhohn & Strodtbeck, 1961). John Spiegel extended the application of value orientations to ethnic families (Committee on the Family, 1970). This framework of value orientations has been used extensively. Its major shortcoming lies in the comparisons that researchers have made without regard for socioeconomic factors (although Spiegel originally specified social class differences). Furthermore, the framework lacks a means by which culture may be analyzed as a dynamic or fluid process. As cultural and societal processes condition family life, so does family life change and condition the culture.

To account for the dynamic nature of both culture and the family, three distinctions within any given culture are useful: traditional values, transitional values, and contemporary values. In most ethnic groups, traditional cultural values can be identified in different degrees. Depending on the industrial development of a country, the traditional cultural values may or may not differ significantly from the contemporary values. In regions where there are major differences between traditional and contemporary values, transitional cultural values represent a mixture of some traditional and contemporary traits, which may or may not lead to conflict between the older and younger generations. Differentiating between traditional, contemporary, and transitional values introduces the time dimension and the possibility of cultural evolution.

With this brief discussion of the cultural dimension, we turn to the other parameter of the model: the economic dimension, as defined by the family's means of making a living (production). Certain theorists (Engels, 1884; Reich, 1966; Zaretsky, 1973; Poster, 1978) suggest that the family's ways of making a living largely shape, develop, and determine many cultural norms, arrangements, and values. The basic thesis is that to understand the family one must study it in relation to the means of production.

Engels (1948) applied the method of historical materialism to the family. This resulted in one of the first analyses of the family at different historical periods. The focus for each historical period was the means of production. In the stage of savagery, group marriage or a polygamous family structure was common. Subsequently, with barbarism, the structure changed to the "pairing family" and, with the rise of civilization, the so-called monogamous family structure emerged. Engels (1948) viewed changes in family life as explained by changes in the mode of production. He argued that during savagery the primary mode of subsistence was through consumption of natural products ready for use. In the stage of barbarism, knowledge of cattle breeding and cultivation of crops was developed, increasing productivity. With the onset of civilization a different stage emerged that further developed "natural products, of industry proper" (Engels, 1948, p. 29). At this time, the development of firearms, coupled with changes in property relations, gave rise to monogamous family structure.

For an excellent critique of Engel's analysis, the reader is referred to Eli Zaretsky (1973) and Mark Poster's (1978) work. Zaretsky applies the method of historical materialism to examine structural changes in the contemporary family. Zaretsky studied the public and personal spheres of modern life and explained this division in terms of the effects of capitalism on the family:

> With the rise of corporate capitalism, the family became the major institution in society given to the personal needs of its members. Society divided between the inner and outer world. At one pole, the individual was central and a sometimes desperate search for warmth, intimacy, and mutual support prevailed. At the other pole, social relations were anonymous and coerced; the individual was reduced to an interchangeable economic unit. (Zaretsky, 1973, p. 80)

The above analyses of the family are representative of studies of family structure as they change throughout time (diachronic), with an emphasis on the impact of economic development. Another level of analysis involves the study of phenomena moving or operating at the same time (synchronic). The models of family structure developed by Poster (1978) involve both diachronic and synchronic components, but have pragmatic value for the synchronic analysis of contemporary families.

Poster (1978) presents four distinct family types:

- bourgeois
- aristocratic
- peasant
- working class

The bourgeois family is "defined by authority restricted to parents, deep parental love for children and a tendency to employ threats of withdrawal of love rather than physical punishment as a sanction" (Poster, 1978, p. 177). By contrast, aristocratic families placed little if any value on privacy, "domesticity, maternal care, romantic love, and intimate relations with children" (Poster, 1978, p. 183). Affective ties for children were not focused on their parents but spread over a wide range of adult figures. Marriages were arranged for political power and political alliances rather than on a basis of romantic love. The peasant family structure had diffused patterns of authority and expression of emotional care throughout the community or village. Many adults participated in child rearing functions, and sanctions were typically enforced with physical punishment rather than threats of withdrawal of love. The working class family structure has drastically changed during the last two hundred years. Initially, the working class family was recruited from migratory peasants, and the "industrialized working class developed a family structure under conditions of economic and social distress" (Poster, 1978, p. 190).

The affective patterns of proletarian families of the early 19th century were characterized by lack of attention and supervision by the mother. "[Children were] raised by the street not by the family" (Poster, 1978, p. 193). Authority and affective bonds were similar to those of the peasant families, but working class communities were not self-contained and responded to the economic changes produced by industrialization.

These four types of families are used by Poster to examine families in the contemporary period. He suggests that families "consist of distinct family patterns, each with its own history, each requiring its own set of explanations of origins and change" (Poster, 1978, p. 197). Indeed, if patterns of socialization, affection, and authority are different for different economic groups, then it is clear that we need to move away from conceptions of the family as a homogeneous phenomenon.

The above exposition leads us into an elaboration of the economic dimensions of the proposed model. The family's means of production or systems of work can be used as criteria for the economic parameter. Two divisions emerge: rural and urban family types. Within the rural families, three general work systems may be identified: the large landowners, the small farmers, and migrant families. The urban families are categorized in accord with the suggestions of Poster (1978) as wealthy, middle class (bourgeois), and working class (proletarian). The criterion for identifying the category that defines family structure is the family's specific means of production, and not the income generated. The fundamental question becomes how the family generates an income. Is it generated through factory work, cultivating the land, professional services, or perhaps, through an inheritance?

A GRID MODEL FOR CULTURE AND CLASS

The cultural and economic dimensions discussed above can be summarized as a grid model. Figure 1 yields 18 cells that describe the family in terms of value orientation and economic status at a particular point in time.

Figure 1 Cultural Values and Economic Differences in Urban and Rural Families

		Traditional	Transitional	Contemporary
Urban Families	Wealthy			
	Middle Class			
	Working Class			
Rural Families	Large Land Owners			·
	Small Farmers			
	Migrant Farmers			

There are several advantages to this model:

- It is dynamic in nature, and changes in either value orientation or economic situations may be traced through the cells.
- Because the model makes use of the interactions of both culture and class dimensions, it provides a framework for comparing family processes.
- The economic origins and cultural evolution of a family can be traced through succeeding generations.
- The framework may be used to examine the migration patterns of families and the effects migration may have on cultural values. Families can be studied before and after the migration experience.
- The model is parsimonious and flexible, and it remains true to the complexity of the subject matter.

A disadvantage of the model is that its application rests on a preliminary study of the traditional aspects of the culture in question. Only then can the contemporary values be detected and understood. Furthermore, an analysis of the economic picture of a culture is also necessary to arrive at an accurate description of the interactions. But the model can serve as a general preliminary guide. Specific parameters need to be developed for families from divergent cultures who respond to different economic pressures. For specific application we now turn to the case of Hispanic families.

APPLICATION OF THE MODEL TO THE PUERTO RICAN FAMILY

In this section we use the general parameters described above to develop a more specific model based on the economic complexities and cultural diversity of a particular Hispanic group—the Puerto Rican family.

Puerto Rico has always been under the influence of a powerful nation. In 1898 the control of the United States was substituted for the control of Spain. The average income in Puerto Rico is below the United States poverty level. The class distinction is as follows: 60% of the families are working class ($4,000 annual income); 30% of the families are middle class; and 10% are wealthy (Informe Estadistico del Departamento de Estado del Govierno de Puerto Rico, 1974). Thus, Puerto Rican family values must be understood in the context of their culture: a heterogeneous, complex, and stratified society dominated by a more powerful nation.

Contemporary Puerto Rican society is not homogeneous. It comprises numerous regional and class co-cultures* (Fernández-Méndez, 1970). Nevertheless, characteristics of the Hispanic heritage lend uniformity to the insular culture. These characteristics include, for example, the use of Spanish language, large families, and the double standard in sexual behavior.

Cultural Value Orientation

A number of writers have described ideal traditional Hispanic values within a Puerto Rican context (e.g., Nieves Falcón, 1972; Garcia-Preto, 1982). For our purposes, we will focus on four key areas that highlight traditional cultural value orientations and have economic implications:

- dependence
- theory of sacrifice
- *respeto*
- machismo and the cult of virginity

Dependence

Generally speaking, children are not believed to be capable of acting independently until they reach "maturity." This maturity is postponed

---

*The term co-culture is used here, rather than subculture, to avoid the hierarchical implications of the latter term (Clark, 1959; Lewis, 1959).

regardless of the physical and emotional development of the child. The conceptualization of children as incapable beings leads to parental over-concern for keeping them close and attached to the family through the process of socialization and limiting their physical mobility (Nieves Falcón, 1972). Dependence is inculcated in children through disciplinary techniques and the theory of sacrifice. As we will see, it is possible that cooperation or dependence may be a value that is shaped according to the culture's priorities, but it may also correspond to one's position in the economic system.

Theory of Sacrifice

In the theory of sacrifice the parents are viewed as being obliged to make all kinds of sacrifices for their children, to the extreme of "giving them our own being." As a response to these sacrifices, their offspring are expected to show gratitude by assuming responsibility for the younger brothers and sisters and/or for the parents in old age. The theory of sacrifice is typically personified in the mother—a good mother makes sacrifices for her children "until death." This relationship between the mother and her offspring is manifested through word and action (Nieves Falcón, 1972). This dependence between parents and children is consonant with a traditional, agricultural society, where children are a potential source of labor. The centralization of power in one figure, namely the father, makes sense in a strongly traditional environment where time is conceived as static and the outside world as hostile. Also, dependence upon the family ensures little social mobility; this was characteristic of the Hispanic system, which enforced social distance and marked class differences.

Respeto

For Puerto Rican families, *respeto* (respect) is one of the most important aspects of interpersonal relations. The word is used across all classes in Puerto Rico. All the disciplinary techniques and valued attributes of dependence, obedience, passivity, and control of aggression are developed as a function of respect, the core of personality traits. The concept of respect also implies social distance. Learning respect, the child learns the behaviors that are considered appropriate in relating to other members of society, according to sex, age, and socioeconomic differences. The father is responsible for the respectful behavior of his children, and he feels morally responsible for the behavior of the whole family (Nieves Falcón, 1972).

Because of the mother's passive role in other aspects of family life, it is hard for the children to see her as an authority figure. She often relies on the father—a strict and authoritarian figure—to enforce compliance. In this way, the father is ever present in the home. The mother is the one who teaches respect for the father. The child who does not show respect is severely censured by the parents and makes the family an object of criticism from the entire community. Through the development of the concept of respect the child learns his or her position in the socioeconomic hierarchy and the form and concept of intra-familial relations and relationships with officials of different institutions in the community. In this way, the child internalizes roles (e.g., rich vs. poor people, female vs. male, and boss vs. employee) and learns to respond to adult demands (Nieves Falcón, 1972).

Machismo and the Cult of Virginity

The notion that children should relate to adults submissively and according to the adults' norms fits well with the female role, generating stability and few contradictions with other societal requirements (Nieves Falcón, 1972). However, the concept of a child as submissive is incompatible with the male role. A boy should be aggressive and daring, but at the same time a "good" boy should be submissive. These contradictions generate anxieties, insecurities, and frustrations in males. The mother will, on the one hand, reinforce obedience and passivity and, on the other hand, encourage aggressiveness and boldness. This long, close, and contradictory relationship between the mother and the male can result in a psychologically dependent man, who uses criteria such as traditions and emotions to make decisions (Nieves Falcón, 1972).

A closer analysis suggests that this apparent contradiction fits with the society's values as a whole. If males are constantly frustrated throughout their childhood due to contradictory expectations, the society is ensuring the reproduction of an aggressive, bold, but irrational man who often attempts to assert his power and virility (machismo). The process is both a vicious cycle and a self-fulfilling prophecy. In this way, the culture perpetuates two of its basic complementary pillars: the cult of virginity and machismo.

The cult of virginity gives rise to severe restrictions regarding females' freedom, keeping the economic and political fields in the hands of males. This arrangement is typical of traditional agricultural societies where Catholicism and a sociology of prestige converge.

According to Fernández-Méndez (1970), machismo is a compensation for the fact that males in Hispanic culture develop insecurely with a great deal of dependence and inferiority feelings resulting from maternal overprotection and disciplinary measures. But he also suggests that machismo could be the only option of affirmation for poor classes where economic, political, and cultural means of affirmation are not possible. Few men in Puerto Rico control or affect any meaningful aspect of the welfare of the island. In other words, men are not in command of their own country. It is possible that machismo, which was deeply rooted in the Hispanic culture, now serves other purposes that are economic and political in nature, such as the alienation and exploitation of a sector of the labor force.

Economic Factors: Means of Production

There are two basic types of families: The rural and urban family. Within the urban family three main subtypes can be identified: the upper class or wealthy families, the middle class family, and the urban proletariat or working class family. The rural families can also be subdivided into three regional cultures, identified by their association with the production of tobacco, coffee, or sugar cane. Although these crops do not play a major role in Puerto Rico's contemporary economy, attitudes and values in the rural family were shaped by them, and their influence remains today (Steward, 1972; Fernández-Méndez, 1970). The family corresponds in its structure and operation with the special needs of the primary means of production (Fernández-Méndez, 1970), both in rural and urban areas. The structure of the family flows from the means of production and not vice versa. For example, a university teacher and a skilled industrial worker may earn the same level of income. However, the structure and quality of life for both will be a function of flexibility or rigidity of the work schedule, as well as other resources available. The family patterns and life styles of a university teacher may be characterized by more leisure time for the family and children, time for cultural and recreational activities available through the university, and special educational resources. In contrast, the skilled worker will have less time for the family because of a fixed schedule and fewer educational resources, etc. These differences in life style condition the structure and function of the family.

Families of the Rural Cultures

The community of the tobacco culture is mainly formed by small rural landowners, and the main goal of each farmer is the maintenance of the family's economic independence (Fernández-Méndez, 1970). This is possible because of the father's exclusive control over the family labor force and severe restrictions with regard to the consumption of food, goods, and services. The father is in charge of the whole production operation—division of labor, control of family resources, the use of the land, the distribution of the tobacco in the market, the administration of the income, etc.—and the other family members are subjected to this ideal of male centrality to keep the family unified. The children are taught to delay personal gratification and to have the family's economic survival as the first priority. We can see here clearly how the development of dependence has many functional reasons (Steward, 1972; Nieves Falcón, 1972).

Formal education is considered "good" but sometimes irrelevant (Nieves Falcón, 1972). Although having an education will ensure better economic conditions, a great deal of the education in these families is provided informally through the family work in the cultivation of the land. School attendance is sporadic because the children work in the fields. Children who grow up in this type of family system, where all personal needs have to be ignored for the fulfillment of the collective needs, may have an atrophied sense of individual independence (Fernández-Méndez, 1970).

The coffee culture family looks upon education somewhat more favorably. Education is the instrument of social and economic mobility. This is the family type with the most members. It is characterized by low income, high fertility index, and a great deal of communal cooperation.

The family from the sugar cane culture lives exclusively on the father's seasonal income and occasional contributions from the mother. The basic economic unit of this sector is the sugar cane plant. The male is taught to tolerate very rough work and to be a good co-worker (compañero) to his equals. Hostilities are generally channeled to the boss and his class (Fernández-Méndez, 1970). The links between the members of this family are weaker than those of the other two types. Marriages break down often and many couples live together without being married. Children in this family do not have any profitable economic role, as in the families of the tobacco and coffee cultures. The child has more freedom and physical mobility within the community. This might be related to some economic factors. The sugar cane industry is based on seasonal crops. Workers are unemployed at least half of the year. This results in additional pressures on the family unit. Migration is frequent, as well as psychosocial problems such as alcoholism. The children are welcomed in most of the neighborhood homes and treated as family members. This gives children a high sense of security within their own culture (Fernández-Méndez, 1970). In the sugar cane culture, education is conceived in realistic terms. The parents would like their children to learn reading, writing, and mathematics but they know that economic opportunities for children of sugar cane workers are very limited (Nieves Falcón, 1972). These three family types have some commonalities. The nuclear family size is generally large. They live in an extended family arrangement, where grandparents, uncles, aunts, and relatives live in the same house or close by. Sometimes the whole neighborhood shares family ties. Cooperation between members of the family and between families is an important attribute, regarded as the main key for the economic and social processes of the community. This spirit of cooperation is taught early to the children (Nieves Falcón, 1972).

Families of the Urban Cultures

In Puerto Rico 65% of the population live in urban centers. There are differences among the three urban family types, and also common features. The urban proletariat, or working class, in Puerto Rico differs from the typical industrial working class. The urban proletariat represents a rural mass that has retained a great deal of its previous rural cultural heritage (Fernández-Méndez, 1970). It is in this class (and the middle class) that the most radical sociocultural changes have occurred. There is a high degree of interaction between households, although the relations between parents and children are not affectively as intense as in the rural context. The physical mobility of children is high and it is reinforced. Parents expect their children to be educated and to improve their social status, although they are aware of the difficulties they will encounter in the process (Nieves Falcón, 1972). These changes suggest a move toward more independence and autonomy for the children (Mussen & Beytagh, 1968). This is understandable if we keep in mind that these families presumably improved their lives through social and economic mobility. There is clearly a relationship between individual independence and social change. Parents are aware that their children need the skills to deal successfully with a new competitive and individualistic environment.

The working class family is relatively new in Puerto Rico. It emerged as a result of the industrialization and urbanization introduced by the United States. Marriages in the working class are affected significantly more than in other cultures by divorce or death of the husband. Women in this culture are more independent in taking care of themselves and their children without male help than in any other culture (Fernández-Méndez, 1970). Attitudes toward education, sex, and work remain more or less the same as in the rural culture. Feeding, hygiene, recreation, discipline, and parent-children relations also remain similar to their counterparts in rural culture. The values of these family work systems are often organized around a focus on reality considerations—the reality principle.

Industrialization and urbanization have created a new social and economic life style in Puerto Rico best represented by its more concrete social manifestation—the urban middle class. The middle class in the big cities of Puerto Rico, as well as the wealthy families, progressively corresponds to the family type characteristic of modern industrialized societies.

This family is typically small, constituted by the parents and their few children. As a result of the accelerated pace of life in the industrialized urban centers, the functions associated with the typical rural family have been delegated to a complex institutional system. Instead of taking care of their old members, the family sends them to nursing homes. Rather than having babies at home, mothers go to specialized hospitals. The idea behind the creation of nursing homes, hospitals, kindergartens, cafeterias, summer camps, banks, and cooperatives is that these will be more efficient. In turn, the provision of services encourages an increasing degree of consumption. Education is highly regarded in this culture as a means of achieving social mobility and status. Parents strongly emphasize higher education.

Just as the reality principle serves as an organizing concept for working class families, the performance principle performs this function for the middle class. The middle class family imitates the wealthy class by ostentatiously displaying their possessions and values (Fernández-Méndez, 1970). This is in conflict with the traditional family values (like "familismo") that are rooted in the agricultural culture. The machismo and cult of virginity, characteristic of the rural cultures and the Hispanic heritage, are shared in varying degrees by the middle class families. In sum, the urban culture is in constant vacillation between the old Hispanic-traditional-agricultural heritage and the new Anglo-consumeristic-industrial influence.

The wealthy have many traits in common with the middle class, but there are some additional features. Higher education for these families is a requirement; it is a necessary aspect in the children's development. The children of wealthy families invest a great deal of their time in art, music, and dance lessons. These lessons will provide them with the friends and social experiences so important for their future lives. The families are more flexible than the middle class families concerning eating habits, toilet training, and sexuality (Nieves Falcón, 1972). The organizing concept for these family systems is the pleasure principle. In general, these cultures, especially the middle class and working class cultures, are harder to describe because their emergence is relatively recent (Inclán, 1978).

THE CALIFORNIA RICANS: A PUERTO RICAN FAMILY IN FAMILY THERAPY

In this section we will attempt to describe how the model in Figure 2 may be useful in the study of families to evaluate the migration process, cultural conflicts, economic mobility, and cultural transitions, and to understand the intergenerational roots of behavioral patterns. Figure 2 incorporates cultural and economic issues that are specific to Puerto Ricans.

The model may be used to examine the same or similar processes with families from anthropological (e.g., Lewis, 1959; Lewis, Lewis, & Rigdon, 1978) and literary (e.g., Márquez, 1963; García-Márquez, 1972) studies. Or it can be used with clinical cases as we do here.

>The Marin family is of Puerto Rican background, and they have been living in northern California for most of their lives. Their great-grandparents and grandparents were born in Puerto Rico. The parents were born outside of Puerto Rico (California and Hawaii), and the children were born in California.
>
>Shortly after the United States intervened in Puerto Rico in 1898, the great-grandparents of both Mr. and Mrs. Marin participated in the so-called "dollar line" program. This was an effort initiated by the United States to relocate labor forces from Puerto Rico to Hawaii for the purpose of developing the Hawaiian sugar industry. This large colony of Puerto Ricans in Hawaii, upon becoming a disenfranchised group, gravitated to California.
>
>Generations ago, the Marin family's basic means of production was the cultivation of sugar. This legacy was continued in Hawaii by the great-grandparents and grandparents, who subsequently migrated to Califor-

Figure 2 Cultural Values and Economic Differences in Puerto Rican Families

		Traditional	Transitional	Contemporary
Urban Families	Wealthy			
	Middle Class			
	Working Class			
Rural Families	Tobacco			
	Coffee			
	Sugar			

nia, joining the migrant farm workers there. Years later, the next generation, those born in Hawaii and/or California, left the fields and moved to the city. Here a shift is made from rural to urban setting. Some of these economic aspects are reflected in the family's genogram. For example, Mr. Marin never knew his biological father until adulthood. He was raised by his mother and a stepfather. At the age of eight, he discovered that he was an adopted child and his other three brothers had different fathers. Mrs. Marin's family shows a similar pattern. She has four siblings and three of them have different fathers. These disrupted genograms have their roots in the economic reality of a family whose means of production was the sugar crop. Because sugar is a seasonal crop, the father either is unemployed for half of the year or he is forced to migrate. The result is often a family with a male absent for extended periods of time—six months or more. The economic pressures, as well as the lowered level of cohesion due to father's prolonged absences and the lack of a unifying family task, often result in disrupted marriages and remarriages. Such a structure contrasts sharply with that of a family connected to the production of coffee or tobacco; these families have relatively intact genograms.

In applying the model to the Marin family, it becomes clear that the early generations (great-grandparents and grandparents), who were Puerto Rican born, belonged to a rural sugar producing family with traditional values. The next generation (parents), born in California (mother) and Hawaii (father), moved to an urban working class level. The values continue to be traditional but they have incorporated more middle class Anglo values than the previous generations did. This generation is able to speak some Spanish, and the preparation of food is done in the Puerto Rican tradition. The younger generation moved the family to a middle class or lower middle class level, with the value structure moving from transitional to contemporary. The children have achieved some degree of higher education. One daughter works as a technician-professional and two other children are in college. This generation is more future- and achievement-oriented and does not speak Spanish.

The Marin family's socioeconomic heritage can be traced intergenerationally in one dimension of the grid model. The other dimension of the model, cultural values, was important in engaging the family in therapy.

The second oldest of four siblings was brought to a psychiatric emergency room with the chief complaint of "I can't function on the outside. I can't take care of myself." This 21-year-old woman had been repeatedly hospitalized since age 16 and had taken a number of psychotropic medications. The young woman was described as well groomed, but depressed, withdrawn, and dependent. Her mood was described as sad. Her thoughts were focused on helplessness and suicidal ideation with concerns over cleanliness.

At the time of the first family interview, Mr. Marin was 47 years old and had been unemployed for the past eight months and Mrs. Marin was 45 years old and unemployed. The oldest daughter was 27 years old and worked as a technician in a health care facility. The second oldest was the identified patient. The third was the only son, who was 17 years old and was completing high school.

During the first interviews it was necessary to discern the family's values in order to evaluate the family and provide effective treatment. With the Marin family respeto (respect), confianza (trust), and sacrificio (sacrifice) were key concepts that facilitated the family's engagement in therapy as well as a shift from individual notions of illness to relationship concerns. For example, during the first family meeting it was clear that a number of family members would become "sick" at different points in time. This was acknowledged by the therapist who commented on how everyone in the family had made great sacrifices. One of these sacrifices has been the symptomatic daughter's attempt to rescue the parents from marital difficulties. The erosion of respect and trust were other issues around which the family engaged in treatment.

During the course of therapy, the focus shifted from the symptomatic daughter to the parents' marital difficulties, and subsequently to the parents' relationship to their own parents. The parents began to work on issues of trust and respect not only in their marriage but in terms of rebalancing debts in their family of origin. In examining the parents' family of origin, a number of cultural and economic patterns surfaced. For example, Mrs. Marin at one point expressed her belief that Puerto Ricans were "stupid" because they did not let their women work. She recounted her experience in Hawaii and explained that the Japanese were "smarter" than the Puerto Ricans, in that everyone participated in some aspect of the work. The men cut the sugar and the women picked it up. By contrast, Puerto Rican men insisted on having their women remain at home. She believed that this was the reason why the Japanese prospered and the Puerto Ricans in Hawaii did not. This comment connects traditional sex role patterns with productive labor and the family hierarchy. Mother's anecdote served to illustrate how the role of women was conditioned by oppressive cultural and economic legacies in the larger society, but it also served as a metaphor for the position that was held by her and by her daughters.

These dialogues occurred within a supportive family context, and enabled Mrs. Marin to turn to her own mother for more information and support. As she reconnected with her mother, a woman who was elderly and bedridden with diabetes, she was able to renew with her mother a relationship of trust from a position of strength. This served to lift part of the burden from the symptomatic daughter. The family worked on several concrete plans that freed them from the chains of invisible cultural, economic, and familial legacies. They remained in treatment for two years and they were able to reverse a pathogenic family process that had paralyzing effects on their daughter.

The Marin family illustrates some of the ways in which this model for the study of Hispanic families can provide a basis for understanding economic and cultural intergenerational issues. With the use of the model, a family's development may be traced on economic and cultural dimensions. Throughout the generations, the Marin family may be traced in Figure 2 as moving from lower to higher socioeconomic status, and from traditional to contemporary values.

An understanding of the family legacy and the changes that transpired were valuable not only in the engagement phase of family therapy but also during the middle and later phases of treatment. An appreciation of the cultural values and work systems of families can help to identify some of the conditions that give rise to dysfunctional family patterns, and can also facilitate work with families to change some of their conditions.

REFERENCES

Clark, M. *Health in the Mexican American culture: A community study.* Berkeley: University of California Press, 1959.

Committee on the Family. *The case history method in the study of family process.* New York: Group for the Advancement of Psychiatry, 1970.

Engels, F. *The origin of the family, private property and the state.* Moscow: Progress Publishers, (1884)/1948.

Fernández-Méndez, E. *La identidad y la cultura.* San Juan: Instituto de Cultura Puertorriquena, 1970.

García-Márquez, G. *Cien años de soledad.* Buenos Aires: Editorial Sudamericana, 1972.

Garcia-Preto, N. Puerto Rican families. In M. McGoldrick, J. Pearce, J. Giordano (Eds.), *Ethnicity and Family Therapy.* New York: Guilford, 1982.

Inclán, J. Socio-economic changes in Puerto Rico: The development of the modern proleterian family. Paper presented at the National Hispanic Conference on Families sponsored by the National Coalition of Hispanic Mental Health and Human Science Organizations, Houston, Texas, 1978.

Informe Estadistico del Departamento de Estado del Govierno de Puerto Rico. San Juan, Puerto Rico; 1974.

Kluckhohn, F.R., & Strodtbeck, F.L. *Variations in value orientations.* Evanston, Ill.: Row, Peterson, 1961.

Lewis, O. *Five families.* New York: New American Library, 1959.

Lewis, O., Lewis, R.M., Rigdon, S.M. *Neighbors: Living the revolution—An oral history of contemporary Cuba.* Chicago: University of Illinois Press, 1978.

Márquez, R. *La carreta.* Rio Piedras, Puerto Rico: Editorial Cultural, 1963.

Mussen, P., & Beytagh, L.   La industrializacion, la crianza del niño y la personalidad infantil." *Revista de Ciencias Sociales,* Vol. XII, Num. 2, 1968.

Nieves, Falcón, L. *Diagnóstico de Puerto Rico.* Rio Piedras: Editorial Edil, 1972.

Poster, M. *Critical theory of the family.* New York: The Seabury Press, 1978.

Reich, W. *Sex-Pol: Essays 1929-1934.* New York: Random House, 1966.

Steward, J.H. (Ed.), *The people of Puerto Rico: A study in social anthropology,* Urbana: University of Illinois Press, 1972.

Zaretsky, E. *Capitalism, the family, and personal life.* New York: Harper & Row, 1973.

4. The Shifting Family Triangle: The Issue of Cultural and Contextual Relativity

Celia Jaes Falicov, PhD
University of California, San Diego

San Diego Family Institute
San Diego, California

Lilyan Brudner-White, PhD
Division of Social Sciences
University of California, Irvine
Irvine, California

The authors wish to thank Braulio Montalvo, Froma Walsh, Monica McGoldrick, and Douglas Breunlin for their comments and suggestions.

A FAMILY CAN BE CONCEPTUALIZED AS A COMPLEX NETWORK OF triangles, some flexible and changing, others rigid and constant, some central, others peripheral, many benign, others malevolent. Triangles have fascinated observers of the human condition across centuries. Malevolent triangles have played key roles in human drama, and have been portrayed in ancient Greek tragedies, the classic plays of Shakespeare, and contemporary literature. They fascinate us because they are a part of the universal human experience. In studying them we learn a great deal about the principles of interaction that shape outcomes in human relationships.

Triangles are pivotal constructs in the field of family therapy. Ties can take the form of alliances, or positive, dyadic supportive relationships; of triangles, as when a third member is included in the interaction between two people; or of coalitions, as when two parties are covertly allied against or excluding a third party. Symptoms of family distress are regularly linked to the presence of family triangles and coalitions (Ackerman, 1966; Bowen, 1972; Haley, 1967, 1976; Minuchin, 1974, 1978; Satir, 1967). A central hypothesis in family therapy is the notion that triangular processes detour from or block the emergence of underlying marital conflict or parental disagreements. Presumably, the very presence of a triangle signals marital tensions. Implicit in many theoretical descriptions of what is pathogenic about these coalitions is the idea that the intrusion of a third party in unresolved marital conflicts reflects these conflicts, and in turn weakens necessary boundaries around the marital dyad and further precludes the resolution of marital discord. Moreover, since the parental alliance is broken, the leadership structure of the family is said to be eroded when the triangular arrangements persist.

Consequently, when therapists note the presence of a triangle they tend to automatically consider strengthening (directly or indirectly) the boundary around the marital pair and attempt to resolve the marital conflict or parental disagreement. This classical intervention may reduce conflict, establish a workable leadership alliance and provide a situation that frees up children caught in the middle of the nuclear unit. But in other families, placing strong boundaries around the marital pair (thereby explicitly or implicitly making the marriage the central focus of therapy) may conflict with other important family values or it may create a strain in the wider social field by undermining other central ties. A coalition may be linked to a problematic marital bond in one kind of family system, but a similar coalition may occur in systems where a close, strong and intimate marital bond is not essential to the good functioning of the family. Similarly, the presence of a triangle does not necessarily signal weakened domestic authority where the leadership

52

structure of the family does not depend upon achieving a strong parental consensus.

Just as individual behavior cannot be understood apart from its immediate context, triangular patterns of interaction cannot be isolated from their cultural context, reified and assumed to have the same universally problematic implications. As Bateson has stated, "the meaning and function of an event is not contained in itself, but in its relation to the context." Hoffman (1981) has also recently questioned the universal pathological implications of cross-generational coalitions. She proposed that different "strain lines" or relationship dilemmas may stem from different cultural family arrangements and suggested the use of anthropological literature to support her argument.

The purpose of this article is to explore the notion that triangles take on their meanings and implications, at least in part, from the cultural context in which they are embedded. We will examine and compare the emergence of coalitions in families governed by different cultural values concerning the nature of the marital relationship and the relationship between the generations. Particular attention is paid to the central emphasized relationships in the nuclear and extended family and the principles of organization that could alter the meaning and function of triangles. These family contexts and their ideologies regarding crucial structural features, such as boundaries and hierarchies, need to be taken into account when assigning dysfunction and planning treatment interventions to change coalitional patterns. It is likely that the criteria that family therapists utilize to assess and intervene in dysfunctional coalitions mirror several core cultural assumptions of the white middle class American nuclear family in terms of how family ties are balanced. A richer theoretical and technical vocabulary regarding triangles may be necessary to accommodate families of different ethnic backgrounds and social classes, or even nuclear families that do not fit the societal ideal.

VARIATIONS IN FAMILIES

Families are cultural organizations and, as such, they vary considerably in their ideologies and principles of organization in different parts of the world. In industrial, technologically advanced, western societies the standard ideal to which many families more or less conform is the isolated middle-class nuclear family. But even in the United States this is only one of several kinds of family systems. Many nuclear families are embedded in various ways and to various degrees in extended family networks that were the prevalent type of organization in the preindustrial or traditional settings. Various ethnic groups and many of the working class and poor sectors of American society live in or are in transition from extended families. The roots of these variations are manifold and range from fundamental survival issues, job opportunities, and division of labor to a traditional emphasis that favors connections with the extended family as a definition of family life, as it occurs in many ethnic groups.

Despite the widespread persistence and adaptive value of extended family ties for many groups, the emphasis in the field of family therapy (and in the dominant culture) has been on developing models of family function and dysfunction that fit the characteristics of the middle-class white nuclear family. Even those models of family therapy that include exploration and change of relationships with the family of origin operate on the ideal values of the nuclear family, since their primary aims are to increase autonomy and self-differentiation or resolve loyalty issues that are impeding the functioning of the nuclear family unit and the marital dyad in particular.

Much less is known about the ideals and principles of organization of the functional extended family network, nor is it known where the vulnerabilities lie in the extended families that become dysfunctional. In order to correctly assess and treat the problems of nuclear families that maintain geographic or emotional proximity to their circle of relatives, it is necessary to articulate a conceptual framework that delineates the ideal values and principles of organization in extended and nuclear families.

THE DOMINANT DYAD IN NUCLEAR AND EXTENDED FAMILIES

One way to conceptualize the differences between the nuclear and the extended family is to focus on what Hoffman (1981) has called the "governing dyad." This concept evolves from the work of anthropologist Francis Hsu (1971). He uses the term "dominant dyad" to refer to the central emphasized relationship in a family system. In some cultures the husband-wife tie is the governing dyad, but in other cultures the governing dyad may be father and son, or mother and son, or even brother and brother. No family system gives equal prominence to all potential dyads: some dyads tend to take relative precedence over others and "when a dyad is thus elevated above others, it tends to modify, magnify, reduce or even eliminate other dyads in a kinship group" (Hsu, 1971, p. 9).

A crucial point to understand is that as the dominant or emphasized relationship varies, so do many of the basic principles or attributes upon which family life is based. Most of the attributes (continuity-discontinuity, inclusiveness-exclusiveness, etc.) are present in all family systems—what varies is their relative emphasis. Where the nuclear family is the ideal form there is a pronounced tendency to give prominence to the husband and wife dyad. In contrast, the extended family tends to discourage the elevation of the marital tie above all others because this threatens the ideal of continuity between the generations, a value so central to extended family life (Levy, 1971). Thus, in extended families the dominant relationship is more likely to be placed in an intergenerational dyad than in a husband-wife dyad. For example, in Chinese and Middle-Eastern traditional families the dominant dyad is father-son, in traditional Hindu society the dominant dyad is mother-son, and in some African societies, it is brother-brother (Hsu, 1971).

Other important differences that affect the functioning of the nuclear family in these two types of arrangement relate to issues of inclusiveness of others and issues of authority and leadership. The husband-wife tie has a special sense of exclusiveness and therefore the inclusion of others can be a potential threat. In the intergenerational arrangement, there is much greater tolerance for inclusiveness of others in the nuclear family. In the husband-wife dominant tie there is little emphasis on the authority of some people over others, while the superordination of one parent is an essential attribute of families based on intergenerational dyads, as in the case of the Chinese traditional family.

Many of these differences are revealed in the treatment situation, for instance, in the way family problems are handled or the degree of tolerance of outsiders in the resolution of problems. However, for the purpose of examining the appearance and regulation of coalitions in each type of family arrangement we will concentrate on two basic structural dimensions, the boundaries and hierarchies that organize the marital dyad and the relationship between the generations.

DOMINANT DYADS AND RULES ABOUT BOUNDARIES AND HIERARCHIES

A closer examination of the attributes characteristic of families based on husband-wife centrality and those based on intergenerational centrality allows us to deduce their implicit rules regarding inclusion and exclusion (boundaries) and leadership and authority lines (hierarchies).

Nuclear Isolated Units

Let us first consider nuclear family units based on the husband-wife dominant tie. When a marital pair joins of their own volition, presumably based on romantic love and exclusive sexuality, this situation introduces an element of fragility and potential discontinuity into a family (particularly in a culture where divorce is common). To protect the family, subsystem boundaries must be clearly marked and closely guarded because the very existence of the family depends on the quality of this tie. As the anthropologist Bohannon (1971) states:

> When something goes wrong in a neolocal nuclear family, it is likely to be either a difficulty in the husband-wife relationship or to depend for its repair on that relationship. Parentage depends on successful marriage—and the usual obverse is that a successful marriage depends on successful parenting. (p. 45)

Husband-wife emotional distance, prolonged separations, and disclosure to third parties and other types of boundary crossing that interfere with the unity and communication of the couple are detrimental to the isolated nuclear family.

The leadership and authority structure of the family is dependent upon reaching parental agreement rather than following predetermined guidelines. Ideally, the sexes are equivalent (although not necessarily equal in function) in parenting, and therefore husband and wife expect joint domestic authority and leadership. Parental consensus needs to be obtained within a context of values that leans toward symmetry among members. Spouses expect equal affective involvement with and rights over the children. A child is expected to love and to be loyal to both parents equally. In the case of divorce, children generally go with the mother, but the outcome cannot be predicted entirely in advance since it in part depends on the quality of the relationship between a child and each parent. Fierce custody battles are a testimony to the egalitarian nature of American parenthood.

In nuclear families children have considerable power and influence. There is a tendency to make colleagues out of children (Bohannon, 1971; Satir, 1967) as parental authority virtually withers away as children advance in age. These life cycle transitions may not be clearly agreed upon by family members and may lead to a situation in which offspring test and polarize parents, sometimes increasing the parental disagreements and conflicts over family hierarchies.

In this and many other areas of family life, the couple in the husband-wife dominant dyad arrangement need to arrive at a reasonable and mutually satisfactory quid pro quo through many implicit and explicit negotiations. Marital pairs who succeed may reap great rewards, but such negotiations offer by their very possibilities considerable sources of family conflict. The expectation is that husband-wife negotiations will favor a family balance that reflects equidistance between each parent and each child, both in terms of affective proximity and in terms of equal respect or acceptance of parental authority.

In the husband-wife dominant dyad arrangements there are no clear traditional rules as to how the three generations are integrated. Each family is left to negotiate its relationship with its families of origin, given that in a highly mobile society the costs vs. benefits of relatives vary depending upon the circumstances of each particular family. Although many outcomes are possible from these negotiations there seems to be an implicit ideal expectation of equidistant laterality, that is, that both husband and wife should give equal treatment to each side of the family. Too much closeness with or inclusion of relatives from the husband's or the wife's side is potentially problematic because it may lead to a lack of clarity of subsystem boundaries and unclear lines of obligation and authority. Thus, there seems to be an ideal isomorphism between the internal organizing principles of the nuclear unit and those that organize their relationship to the kinship network.

Nuclear Units as Part of Extended Family

The nuclear family embedded in an extended network is on a wholly dissimilar field of social interaction, wired to a different circuit of communication. The importance of the nuclear family is somewhat diminished and the boundary around the marital couple less clearly marked. Subsystem boundaries often follow a sexual division of labor. Women are the unit of cooperation in many tasks and men in others. Both men and women relate intimately with members of the same sex within the extended network. In her classic study of English families, Bott (1957) found that a large and dense social network usually meant clear role segregation between husband and wife and fewer demands placed on the spouse for intimacy and assistance in a variety of tasks. Similarly, Komarovsky (1967) in her study of working class American families found marital conflict to be minimized because the couple does not make joint decisions, nor is it the sole problem-solving center of the family. Not only are fewer demands placed on the marital partner when other adults are around, but when something goes wrong in a marriage the difficulties may be repaired by mediators or assuaged by confidants, particularly when divorce is not a common practice. Rules of inclusion/exclusion of others in marital subsystem issues appear to be more flexible than in the middle class nuclear family.

Leadership and authority are vested in the intergenerational tie. In the case of the father-son dominant dyad family, the executive power rests with the father who eventually passes it to the son (although in these systems women may also obtain power and authority with age). At least publicly, father is the ultimate authority, while mother's power is considerably smaller. Father's functions and mother's functions tend to be complementary rather than symmetrical. In a study of Mexican villages, Hunt (1971) noted that patterns of children's siding sometimes with mother and sometimes with father were quite typical and viewed as appropriate given the division of labor and the functional differences in the role of mother and father. In the relationship between parents and children, the balance tilts toward more complementarity than symmetry. Children respect the parents' hierarchical position throughout life and move very slowly from a position of inequality toward. greater equality (Clark & Mendelson, 1975).

Siblings, cousins, and many other relatives play important roles for each other throughout life. Often in intact extended families there are some guidelines to follow regarding the integration of the three generations; the most obvious are those relating to patrilocal or matrilocal descent and residence. Extended families, in contrast to the nuclear units, are based on asymmetry in the distribution of power and do not seem to require affective equidistance among members. In the traditional Chinese family, for instance, the father-son dyad is given prominence by means of a built-in, traditionally "solved" distribution of power, which excludes women from the start. On the other hand, greater affective closeness between mother and children may be culturally sanctioned.

Among other things, these organizing principles may facilitate or constrain the formation of certain kinds of alliances and coalitions, through rules and metarules about who is in charge, who is included and who is kept out. Each type of family arrangement seems to generate predictable triangular processes, and even predictable attitudes toward certain triangles.

TRIANGULAR PROCESSES IN NUCLEAR AND EXTENDED FAMILIES

The emphasis on a particular governing dyad creates a set of rules regarding who should relate to whom and in what manner. These rules could be said to be a sort of "cultural code." As Sluzki (1975) notes, "in the human species, the socialization process includes the transmission of a huge code" (p. 67). This code includes rules or metarules about how the relationships should be interpreted, defined, or negotiated.

Cultural codes need to be taken into account for many types of family triangles, from extramarital affairs to grandparent-grandchild coalitions. Furthermore, the same "shape" of a triangle, for example a cross-generational coalition, may function one way in one type of family arrangement and quite another way in a family based on different cultural principles. The meaning and function of a coalition may *shift* depending on the cultural context.

Triangulation of children may be a stop-gap measure for nuclear families in distress. Since prolonged separations or excessive marital distance are very problematic, "triangulated" children can help reduce the distance by providing a mutual focus of concern or by involving the peripheral parent. Marital dissatisfaction and unresolved marital disagreements pose a major threat to the continuity and the authority structure of the nuclear family. Since, ideally, children are equally attached to mother and to father, if one parent enlists the cooperation of a child in a marital struggle, or if the child becomes more sympathetic toward one parent, such loss of equidistance can be construed as an attack on the excluded parent and thus unbalance the family system. It is easy to see that a cross-generational coalition strikes at the foundation of the nuclear family and therefore it is not surprising that many of these triangles remain covert. The metarules about acknowledgment of coalitions may also be part of the code.

Identical coalitionary processes are common and observable in nuclear families living in extended settings but they probably do not have the same unbalancing effect. Lines of authority are clearly defined a priori and exclusion is not read as attack where marital satisfaction and parental consensus are not essential for continuity. In father-son dominant dyad systems, mother's low position (from our view) in the family's hierarchy may prompt her to form a coalition with the son, either to challenge the father through the son, or simply because a relationship with the son may be one of the few avenues of closeness with the husband. However, these efforts at a coalition do not immediately incur danger. A father who is culturally secure in his parental leadership could probably dismiss his wife's complaints about him to the son as a woman's weakness or chattiness and not regard it as a threat. It is likely that the rest of the family, including the wife, will regard this triangular arrangement as unsatisfactory, but basically benign or "traditional," as in the case of the "hausfrau" of the German patriarchal household (Slater, 1977) who publicly endorses the father's authority while privately siding with the children. The children may indeed feel more distant from father than from mother but still respect his authority. In fact, many children in patriarchal families feel that enlisting mother's cooperation may be the only way to obtain some privileges and handle father's strictness. Equidistance is not expected and authority is not as fragile when the nuclear family lives enveloped by the extended network.

Therefore, cross-generational triangles shift in meaning and impact in extended families, compared with nuclear ones. If the intergenerational, and not the marital tie is supposed to be the central one, then cross-generational coalitions involving children can be given other meanings. Haley (1967) suggests that a wife may join a child against her husband as a way of maintaining distance from her husband because an intimate relationship with her husband will have repercussions in her relationship with her own parents and even in the parents' marital relationship.

As in opening the range of a lens to see more of the field, when one moves from the level of a small social unit to a larger group, the meaning of events shifts. In the larger social field of the extended family, the constellation of ties that is likely to upset the family balance is different because the intergenerational tie is central. Threats to its continuity and hegemony need to be severely countered. In a father-son or mother-son dominant dyad system, parents may react to the new-found closeness of a son with a peer group or with a girlfriend or wife by viewing it as an attack on family solidarity.

In extended networks, the permeable boundaries around the nuclear family allow frequent inclusion of adult siblings or other relatives. They can fulfill many instrumental functions, reduce tensions and diffuse conflict. Many alliances may be acceptable, particularly when they follow sex lines. But some same-generational alliances may also threaten the balance of the nuclear family, as when an adult sibling moves in and over time forms a coalition with one spouse (usually his or her sibling) against the other (Falicov & Karrer, 1980).

Same generational coalitions may indeed have dangerous implications for systems based on intergenerational centrality (Hoffman, 1981). These coalitions arise, for instance, from marriages in which the husband supports the wife to disengage from her overbearing mother or the wife wins the husband over from his attachment to his mother. These are functional processes from the vantage point of the marital dyad but may be very disturbing for families based on intergenerational ties.

Undoubtedly, we know much less about extended families and what types of triangles can enter into conflict in those arrangements. Our hypotheses are based on anthropological, sociological, and clinical observations, but more research is needed to ensure that we are not comparing unstable nuclear families with stable extended systems or unstable extended systems with stable nuclear families.

It would appear then, that cross-generational coalitions are particularly troublesome and may lead more readily to "structural faults" in the middle class nuclear family, given the ideological principles upon which it is based. A cross-generational coalition does not fit or it is incongruent with the ideals of marital unity, parental equidistance from children and egalitarian hierarchies. Coalitionary processes identical in form (and perhaps arising in part from similar "cause," such as marital dissatisfaction) need not have the same impact on families that do not depend as strongly on well delineated subsystem boundaries for marital continuity and where the leadership structure of the family is not solely dependent upon a strong parental consensus. In families where continuity of generations, complementarity of functions and hierarchical differences are important, same-generation coalitions may be incongruent and therefore become associated with serious relationship problems.

It appears that one of the important intervening variables between a triangular arrangement and the interpretation of dysfunction is the cultural code contained in the organizational principles of family systems. Viewed in this way, triangular arrangements per se are inherently neutral but take on their meaning and implication in part from the underlying cultural code that defines their degree of acceptability. Therefore, the potential for function or dysfunction of a triangle seems to lie, at least in part, in its fit or congruence with the total social field. Since one of the important ways in which families differ is in how the dyadic and triadic patterns fit together, a consideration of the nature of the dominant dyads involved may be a necessary first step in the interpretation of many family triangles.

IMPLICATIONS FOR THERAPY

For purposes of comparison and contrast we have discussed the ideologies and principles of organization of nuclear and extended families as if they were separate and distinct. In reality, all families, including the most traditional, are constantly exposed to modern nuclear family ideologies. And even the most modern have contacts with the families they come from.

Most families partake of, combine, and alternately use the principles of each type of family to develop their own unique rules. In spite of these complex realities of family life, there is a bias in American psychotherapy that favors the husband-wife dyad and regards continued attachment to parents as deviant and immature. In a study of Jewish families living in New York, Rogers and Leichter (1964) found that although 63% of the 137 couples in their study valued continued close contact with both families of origin, only 3% of their therapists approved of so close a tie between parents and older children. In 60% of these cases, the assessment of the therapists would have recommended drawing a tighter boundary around the marital dyad, although this move was considered to be ''against tradition'' and ''selfish'' by their clients.

Since all families contain organizational features and codes relevant to different types of dyad dominance, family assessments should always include an evaluation of the degree and type of insertion of the nuclear unit in the extended network, with a view to discovering the prevailing dominant dyads. The coalitions observed could then be screened through the corresponding cultural code (regarding hierarchies and boundaries) as a first step towards sorting out the culturally acceptable from the dysfunctional triangles. Of course, the triangles that are regularly generated by cultural patterns of family interaction can become dysfunctional depending on the particular family's circumstances. But this screening procedure would help to guard against the tendency to gravitate toward and intervene in those triangles that might imply dangerous cleavages according to the ideals of the dominant culture. This stance implies an acceptance of family variation and a very close examination of the ramifications of triangular arrangements before deciding to intervene. It is important to recognize that some types of families are more open to ''triangling'' others than is considered to be ideal for the American culture, given that in many families sharply delineated boundaries around the husband-wife tie are not expected. The reliance of either the husband or the wife on personal networks, or even the disclosure of marital dissatisfaction to these outsiders is not only common among working class families but, rather than being detrimental, it may enhance the stability of the marriage (Komarovsky, 1967). Triangles involving extended family members are apparently more readily tolerated by poor and working class than by middle class couples, probably because they favor the preservation of intergenerational ties, but also because relatives serve important and necessary functions. Two brief examples illustrate these points in situations where therapists may wrongly respond to the appearance of triangles by strengthening the marital bond.

In an Italian family where the husband is a fisherman at sea for several months a year the benefits of his wife's ties to her mother outweigh the adjustment costs that arise when he returns. Mother and daughter function as allies to keep the daughter's marriage together: mother helps daughter with certain tasks, thus relieving pressure on the daughter's spouse. Among other things, the mother-daughter interactions may include venting complaints about the absent spouse. The cultural background of the family and the husband's occupation may work together to facilitate the continuation of the mother-daughter tie. Circumstances do not permit the strengthening of the parental or marital alliance and blocking the mother from "interfering" in the nuclear family, nor is it advisable to do so.

In Mexico, it is common and culturally valued for men of all socioeconomic levels to be involved with the "amigo system" in which they have important, often lifelong, friendships with other men (DeHoyos and DeHoyos, 1966). These ties begin during adolescence and have many important socializing and socioeconomic functions in a society where jobs and advancement depend on patronage and inside connections. The families of origin are based on the principles of the intergenerational dyad in which parents fully accepted these male friendships. Rather than shifting priorities, many men persist in their associations with the "amigo system" after marriage. This situation can contribute to considerable marital alienation. But wives may resign themselves and rely on "triangling" in a child or relative to accomplish the tasks that in husband-wife dominant dyad families are performed by the husband. "Therapeutic" pressure on the Mexican husband to give up his friends and become closer to his wife or help with tasks may go so strongly against cultural values that it will only create further conflict and serious marital discord.

Many families are in transition from extended to nuclear units through the inevitable changes induced by urbanization, modernization, and migration. Landau and Griffiths (1981) and Landau, Griffiths, and Mason (1982) have described family problems developing from this transitional process along with intervention strategies particularly appropriate to deal with these conflicts.

In our view, the concept of the dominant dyad can be used to conceptualize cultural transitional conflicts. Families who migrate are often faced with the need to resolve the contradictory demands implicit in different dominant dyads' priorities. Migrant families often move from settings where there is stability of values and ideals based on tradition, generational continuity, and authority, to rapidly changing settings where the family is based on the centrality of the marital dyad.

Other developmental transitions, such as life cycle events, also create dilemmas over relational priorities that cannot be readily resolved. One fundamental question for a therapist may be whether for families in transition the cultural code includes a metacode, that is, a code about changing the code during crucial transitions. In each case, the questions may be asked, when a couple gets married, moves, has children and so on: Do their rules about boundaries and hierarchies need to change to fit the cultural code regarding centrality of husband-wife dyad (which by definition is discontinuous with the traditional code based on the intergenerational dyad)? Or does their nuclear unit need to be simultaneously congruent with the values of the extended family in which they are embedded? Is there congruence among the different family subsystems in terms of dominant dyad priorities?

Shifts in the dominant dyad priorities can become very problematic when families are faced with multiple, sometimes contradictory adaptational demands. For example, a massive ecological transition such as migration may be compounded by a stressful and apparently contradictory life cycle transition such as parenthood. Family members are usually struggling with changes in cultural code while trying to develop new relationship rules congruent with the new settings. Most families eventually accomplish this task, but some develop symptoms when attempting to force a blend between two contradictory sets of rules. Under these circumstances, a triangle may emerge as an attempted solution to the contradictory demands implicit in different dyad priorities. To intervene in these situations it is important to understand the family's trajectory of migration and acculturation, because this information can provide valuable guidelines regarding which dyads in the system need reinforcement.

In the example that follows, resolving a triangle by strengthening the marital bond appeared to be appropriate to the family's new ecological setting.

A migrant Mexican man became caught in a triangle involving his mother and his wife when he insisted on leaving a baby daughter with his mother, using the principle that "a mother is always a mother and she cannot live without her children." All along, he was unaware of the implications of this statement for the mother of his own child. Rather than a sign of pathology, this widespread pattern of leaving a child in the native land with a grandparent needs to be recognized (and therefore "normalized") as a legitimate attempt to resolve the practical and emotional problems of separation, and to maintain some sense of continuity with the family of origin. The biological mother, who may be culturally used to the idea of patrilocal residence, temporarily accepts the decision to leave her child. Nevertheless, over time she succeeds in her continuous appeals to reincorporate the child into the nuclear family. The reincorporation is stressful, and the child may remain for a long time an emotional link, triangulated between the extended and the nuclear family.

Although adaptive to the immediate circumstances of migration, the decision to leave a child behind can eventually weaken or prevent the formation of a marital bond that by force of circumstance needs to be based on a husband-wife dominant dyad. Since this particular family had made a commitment to remain in this country after two "trial" returns, it was felt that the development of a stronger parental alliance would probably serve this family's goals better than the permeable boundaries with the grandparental generation (which, among other problems, implied a "ping-pong" position for the young child). The parental alliance was encouraged because marital unity would strengthen the family in this setting, not because underlying marital problems were suspected or inferred from the presence of a triangular process. Considerable sensitivity to the cultural background of the family was necessary in order to strengthen the marital bond without challenging the father's traditional prerogatives, and simultaneously making room for the mother's place in the family. The presenting symptom was that the father hit the six-year-old daughter when she repeatedly refused to eat (her mother's food). This act on the part of the father was reframed as a cooperative effort with the mother to have the child act more respectfully and obediently and accept *her* mother's food. The positive interpretation of the father's behavior increased the closeness between husband and wife and this was further reinforced when both parents accepted a suggestion to attend *together* a discussion group on parenting issues for Spanish speaking parents.

Learning from and imitating families, therapists can come to appreciate that the doors between the extended and nuclear family can be selectively and alternately opened and closed by activating, reinforcing, or de-emphasizing different dyads in the service of the situation and the family's particular ecological and cultural setting.

CONCLUSION

Our goal in this paper has been to suggest that the identification of dysfunction in family triangles can only be achieved by knowledge of the particular type of family arrangement. We have explored the conditions under which triangular processes may occur, and become problematic, in nuclear and extended types of families, to open the topic for further comparative study. In the process of doing so, we have become more sharply aware of some of the cultural principles upon which family therapy theories about triangles are based. Undoubtedly, there is a need for further study of function and dysfunction in family arrangements other than the American middle class nuclear family, as well as a metaposition of therapists in relation to their own theories and preferred modes of intervention.

REFERENCES

Ackerman, N.W. *Treating the troubled family*. New York: Basic Books, 1966.

Bohannon, P.J. Dyad dominance and household maintenance. In F.K. Hsu (Ed.), *Kinship and culture*. Chicago: Aldine, 1971.

Bott, E. *Family and social network*. New York: Free Press, 1957.

Bowen, M. Family psychotherapy. *American Journal of Orthopsychiatry*, 1972, *31*, 40-60.

Clark, M., & Mendelson, M. Mexican-American aged in San Francisco. In W.C. Sze (Ed.), *Human life cycle*. New York: Jason Aronson, 1975.

De Hoyos, A., & De Hoyos, G. The Amigo system and alienation of the wife in the conjugal Mexican family. In B. Farber (Ed.), *Kinship and family organization*. New York: John Wiley and Sons, 1966.

Falicov, C.J., & Karrer, B. Cultural variations in the family life cycle: The Mexican American family. In E. Carter & M. McGoldrick (Eds.), *The family life cycle: A framework for family therapy*. New York: Gardner Press, 1980.

Haley, J. Toward a theory of pathological systems. In G. Zuk & I. Boszormenyi-Nagy (Eds.), *Family therapy and disturbed families*. Palo Alto: Science and Behavior Books, 1967.

Haley, J. *Problem solving therapy*. San Francisco: Jossey-Bass, 1976.

Hoffman, L. *Foundations of family therapy*. New York: Basic Books, 1981.

Hsu, F.K. (Ed.). *Kinship and culture*. Chicago: Aldine, 1971.

Hunt, R. Components of relationships in the family: A Mexican village. In F.K. Hsu (Ed.), *Kinship and culture*. Chicago: Aldine, 1971.

Komarovsky, M. *Blue collar marriage*. New York: Random House, 1967.

Landau, J., & Griffiths, J.A. The South African family in transition—Therapeutic and training implications. *Journal of Marriage and Family Therapy*, 1981, 7(3) 339-344.

Landau, J., Griffiths, J., & Mason, J. The extended family in transition: Clinical implications. In Kaslow (Ed.), *The international book of family therapy*. New York: Brunner Mazel, 1982.

Levy, M. Notes on the Hsu hypotheses. In F.K. Hsu (Ed.), *Kinship and culture*. Chicago: Aldine, 1971.

Minuchin, S. *Families and family therapy*. Cambridge: Harvard University Press, 1974.

Minuchin, S., Rosman, B., & Baker, L. *Psychosomatic families: Anorexia nervosa in context*. Cambridge: Harvard University Press, 1978.

Rogers, C., & Leichter, H. Laterality and conflict in kinship ties. In W. Goode (Ed.), *Readings on the family and society*. Englewood Cliffs, N.J.: Prentice Hall, 1964.

Satir, V. *Conjoint family therapy*. Palo Alto: Science and Behavior Books, 1967.

Slater, P. *Footholds*. New York: E.P. Dutton, 1977.

Sluzki, C. The coalitionary process in initiating family therapy. *Family Process*, 1975, *14*(1), 67-77.

5. The Sounds of Silence: Two Cases of Elective Mutism in Bilingual Families

Carlos E. Sluzki, MD
Mental Research Institute
Palo Alto, California

School of Medicine
University of California, San Francisco
San Francisco, California

N = 2 ISN'T TOO MUCH OF A SAMPLE. HOWEVER, THE COMMONALITY shown in two families who consulted the author of this article for a strikingly similar problem leads him to present this communication, as it may resonate with the experience of other therapists working with families in which bilingualism compounds and synthesizes conflicts of loyalties between past and present, between cultures, and between family members.

Both families were referred within a year of each other, presenting as reason for consultation, in both cases, *elective mutism* in a 9-year-old girl. The label " elective mutism" refers to a steady refusal to talk in certain contexts and not in others by a child who has the capability of talking and of understanding circumstances and content of communicative behavior of others, and who otherwise shows a behavior appropriate to age and no signs that may lead the therapist to suspect autism or any other severe disorder of any cause.

What follows is the description of both consultations, their follow-up, and a closing comment.

FAMILY A

Family A consulted the therapist, at the urging of a school psychologist and of a family physician, because the 9-year-old daughter, the only child of this family, had ceased talking at school during the last 6 to 8 months. She had remained totally silent, both with teachers in class and with other children during recess. Otherwise, the child was an average student in school, completing her homework and progressing satisfactorily in terms of her written performance. Their family physician, who inquired about the appropriateness and the format of the consultation, was invited by the therapist to attend. The therapist recommended that all members of the family participate in the interview, which took place in a family-oriented primary care facility in an inner-city general hospital. Present at the consultation were the identified patient, a thin, alert 9-year-old girl; her mother, a 32-year-old Mexican American; her present husband, a 40-year-old Mexican; and the family physician. The overall climate of the interview was cordial. While they entered the room, the therapist actively attempted to engage the girl, who, in turn, rejected him in silence while smiling tensely and maintaining good eye contact. This satisfied his need to screen out, to start with, the display of severe behavior disturbances by the child. The spontaneous sitting arrangement was, clockwise, mother, daughter, family physician, husband (sitting rather separate from the rest), and the therapist. The first contacts included the question, "Who speaks what language at home?" to which the mother answered that she, born and raised in the United States, spoke mainly English, and her husband spoke only Spanish. At home they managed with a mixture of both. The daughter, informed the mother, generally spoke English, to which the husband added, jokingly (in Spanish) "But she also talks pidgin Spanish." The therapist, bilingual himself, decided to tackle from the start what seemed to him a striking family rule that ensured a policy of silence, confusion, or, at least, disinformation, and told them that he would talk to each of them in his/her preferred language, and then would translate whatever was said into the other language, "for the sake of the others." Thus, throughout the interview, the man spoke in Spanish, the woman in English, except for short phrases in Spanish, and the family physician in English. When the reason for consultation was explored, the mother responded that the daughter had progressively ceased talking at school over the last year, and that recently the girl had been talking less and less at home too. In fact, during the last weeks the mother had resorted to talking with the daughter through enacted dialogues with dolls and puppets, which they both seemed to enjoy. The therapist asked whether the father of the girl was in the picture. This question elicited a rather confused answer that could be summarized in the statement "The father lives in the area." The confusion was mainly the result of incomplete phrases in which part of the content was insinuated rather than said by both adults. When asked whether the biological father saw the daughter, the mother commented that she had decided not to favor that, and the husband added: "Well, when he is not mentioned, everything remains calm and peaceful," stressing that the girl and he have a good relationship. The therapist, always translating into English any statements made in Spanish "mainly for the doctor's sake," and into Spanish any statements made in English "for the husband's sake," urged them to expand on the issue, which the mother did somewhat reluctantly, while signaling that she would rather not talk in front of the daughter. The following story ensued: the mother was left by her husband some 5 years ago, and the man established another family in a nearby city. However, each time he would come and pick up the daughter for a weekend visit, he would expect of the wife—and obtain, for quite a while—sexual availability, threatening to withdraw otherwise all economic support and disappear from the daughter's life for good. That situation continued for some 3 years, including the first year of the relationship between the mother and her new man. However, when the latter moved into her house, the mother, no longer totally dependent on her former husband economically (and emotionally), told him firmly that he was welcome to visit the daughter and to take her for weekend outings, but that she would no longer accept him "as husband." Her former husband, however, kept on attempting sexual contact on several occasions, and undermined her standing with the girl—including instructing the daughter not to speak or learn Spanish, the language of the mother's new man. Finally, after one confrontation triggered again by his sexual requirements, the former husband cursed her and left for good, without ever attempting to establish contact with her or with their daughter. The mother decided, in turn, not to attempt to contact the girl's father as she used to do to entice him to visit her. But she considered this policy a failure of her maternal duties, and stated that she was keeping the daughter and her father apart by her inaction. This story was told filled with incomplete phrases and implied meanings. The therapist completed the gaps, as much as he could, with the corresponding explicit words (carefully selected for obvious reasons of modesty, when necessary), adducing his need to be clear "for the sake of accuracy of the translation." The husband remained quite supportive of his wife throughout her storytelling, encouraging her to open up; when she cried at a given moment, he teased her gently: "Look, you are going to appear crying on TV," (referring to their having authorized videotaping). The blatant twist of logic implied in the mother's scenario (she took full responsibility for having separated father and daughter while it was he who established the condition that led to that outcome) completely escaped them. The therapist's reaction to her story, stated almost casually, "Oh, I see, it was *your husband* who decided not to see your daughter unless you acquiesced to his wishes" was met by a silence, a blank face with a slightly furrowed brow, and her "Come again?" The therapist repeated the statement three times in English, following different grammatical forms, and each time the mother looked baffled. The mother switched finally from confusion to "I know, I know." The therapist repeated it twice in Spanish "for the husband's sake." The daughter sat quite still, paying careful attention to the interaction. The mother was praised for her determination to stand up for her own rights, and again she reacted first with bewilderment and then with agreement. In the course of this part of the session, the husband's chair was moved into the circle, and his role as father "for all practical purposes" was stressed. At closure, as the only task proposed to the family, the daughter was requested to teach English to her for-all-practical-purposes-father, which she accepted, nodding. The session was closed and, as the family was escorted out, the daughter broke her silence and uttered with animation to the therapist: "Do you like my new overcoat? I got it for my birthday a week ago." The family was seen for a second and last time, 3 weeks afterwards, and the mother informed that the school had reported a normalization of the behavior of the child. During that interview, they sat equidistantly in a mother-daughter-father order, and they talked about different issues of family life. No new session was scheduled. A 3-month follow-up showed that the daughter passed through a period in which a school teacher complained to the mother that the girl was too talkative and violent with other children, but that also subsided, and a 6-month follow-up showed no new problems in any family member.

Highlights of the first session include

- the rather explicit rules of silence in the family, repeated and enacted many times: "Whatever is not mentioned does not exist"
- the language polarity: if the girl speaks in Spanish, she betrays her father's injunction, and if she does not, she betrays her allegiance to her stepfather as well as her mother's preference
- the skewed allocation of blame in the family history as perceived by the participants, which had defined mother as a villain and the child and her father as victims, leaving very little room for the stepfather

FAMILY B

Family B was referred by a school counselor, who in turn had seen the identified patient once, referred by her teacher. The reason for consultation was once again a 9-year-old girl who, in spite of performing appropriately to her age in terms of social behavior and in written schoolwork, did not speak one word at school—she was a third-grader in a public elementary school in the San Francisco bay area. The appointment was made by the mother, who was invited to confer with the whole family. Present were the mother, a 40-year-old Salvadorian; the father, a 45-year-old Salvadorian, and their only daughter, a 9-year-old who remained silent throughout the interview in spite of efforts of her parents to make her greet the therapist. Two adolescent offspring were not invited by the parents because "they are into other things." The child maintained good contact in spite of her shyness. The mother looked middle class and formal; the father behaved more informally and dressed more humbly. The sitting arrangement was, clockwise, mother, daughter, father (slightly out of the circle), and therapist. Asked about what language they preferred to use in the interview, the father stated, in Spanish, that he had a blockage that made it almost impossible for him to learn English, in spite of the number of years he had lived in the United States. They spoke Spanish at home, even though the mother and daughter frequently spoke English when they were by themselves. The mother spoke English fluently as well as Spanish, and so, the parents said, did the daughter, who was raised in a Latino environment but went to an English-speaking school. The interview was carried on in Spanish with occasional statements in English by the therapist to the daughter (which he then translated into Spanish). When invited to describe the reason for consultation, the parents stated that they conferred at the school's instigation, and were rather dumbfounded about it, as the girl spoke without inhibition at home with them—even though, they added, she had always been a rather silent person. When asked whether they were worried about this problem, both denied it: the father insisted that the girl talked at home, "which is what counts" and the mother commented that she herself was timid and silent at that age, and she outgrew it. When their migratory history was explored, the following story unfolded: they were a middle-class family in San Salvador, where both families of origin live. The woman described herself as very much under her own family's thumb in spite of being married and already having two children. About 10 years ago she decided to go by herself to the United States in order to work and manage by herself, and in that way prove to her father (who had dared her) that she had the capabilities to develop an independent means of life, away from the family's protective umbrella. Without their planning it and not knowing it, during the last weeks before her move she became pregnant. She moved to the States, found a stable job in a factory and when, several months afterwards, she realized that she was in fact pregnant, she decided to stay and so informed her family. In the United States, she explained, she had good health coverage as part of her work health insurance, and, even more important, she was blooming away from what she experienced as the oppressive atmosphere of her family of origin. (The therapist had the educated guess that she might have escaped from an incestuous relationship that her father wanted to maintain, but that hypothesis was not explored in the course of the interview.) She asked her husband to join her and he, agreeing to do so, sold with considerable loss a retail store that he owned in San Salvador. Since his arrival almost 10 years ago he has been unable—due to language limitations, he added—to find any job better than the one he holds now, as a janitor, which he described as stable but utterly uninspiring. She delivered her side of the story with pride and joy, and he his own tale of obvious social and economic descent with a mixture of resentment and resignation. When questioned, following some veiled comments that he made, he stated that he had not made up his mind yet on whether to stay in the United States or to return to his country—to which he had gone back a few times for short visits since their departure. He commented once again about his incapacity to learn English, which considerably damaged his chances of obtaining a better job. The therapist then told the daughter that he was moved by the sacrifice of silence she made to bear witness to her daddy that she was not betraying him by speaking the language of a country that brought him so much bitterness and disappointment, while bearing witness to her mommy that she did not betray her and thus went to school and learned all the many things offered by a country that was so generous and kind to her. (While he made this statement, big tears began to roll silently down the girl's cheeks, and that continued almost to the end of the session.) He also commended the parents for being clear and nonmystifying with their daughter in terms of this dilemma they were confronting between cultures and between themselves as a couple—to which they stated, "But we try not to talk in front of her about all those things," but were reassured by the therapist that they had managed to be clear just the same—and for having reacted with sensitivity to their daughter's plea and agreed to a consultation. This, they were told, probably implied that they felt the responsibility for the management of the problem should once again be in their own hands, and that the daughter had done enough by means of bringing the issue to light. Throughout this long statement, both parents fluctuated between expressing confusion and understanding of what the therapist was saying. The therapist asked the parents how long it would take them to make a final decision whether to stay or return—the question was posed to no one in particular even though the only one with doubts seemed to be the father, and he answered, "Two months." The therapist recommended that the daughter continue in silence for the next 2 months in order to give her father time to decide while reminding him of the need to make a decision. The interview ended with a request that they call back in 2½ months to let the therapist know about the decision and how things were in general. Some 3 months later, not having received a call from the family, the therapist called them and the woman informed him that they had transferred the girl into a bilingual parochial school, where she was doing fine and was quite talkative. No new problems have ensued. A follow-up 6 months later showed no new developments. The father is still in the United States.

Highlights of this sessions are

- the language polarity, tied to a polarity of allegiances, English being positively regarded by the mother and negatively regarded by the father, and the reverse for Spanish and all things associated with it
- a mystified chronic situation in which the man had been in the United States for over 9 years "without making up his mind whether he was there provisionally or to stay"
- glimpses of rules of silence and of "skeletons in the closet" that tend to support these rules

COMMENT

In bilingual people, the choice of language has a symbolic meaning in and by itself—as languages are tied to contexts, memories, experiences, life periods, and relationships. They are clear markers of allegiances as well as reminders of many family rules. The choice of one language over another for a given transaction may automatically establish a boundary by means of including some and excluding other family members, according to their knowledge of the language. The choice of a language may define even the tone or climate of a given situation; for instance, bilingual couples may be found to show a tendency to fight in one language and to converse about neutral subjects in another; there are bilingual families in which discipline is imparted in one language and praise in another; in some of these families the choice of language will define the participants as engaged in a parent-children relationship or in a peer relationship (regardless of the present age of the participants).

Leaving aside stylistic usages, a choice of language activates allegiances, and there are settings and contingencies in which a choice between allegiances becomes untenable—one of the many versions of the "damned if you do, damned if you don't" dilemma: the subject has neither the power nor ability to disobey the injunction *to choose,* nor the luxury of insight; neither the leeway to comment on the untenable nature of the situation, nor the possibility of simply leaving the field. Under those double-binding circumstances and constrictions, the way out is generally a symptomatic solution (cf. Sluzki and Veron, 1971, derived in turn from Bateson et al., 1956). The symptom is a choice of behavior given those circumstances, as these two cases clearly illustrate.

Why this symptom and not another? Even though random events contribute to dictating the selection of symptoms, this process is frequently overdetermined by culture and context. Elements that contribute to that choice include the interpersonal impact of the symptom (i.e., its power to generate behaviors that in turn contribute to maintaining it) and its symbolic value (i.e., the themes it evokes and the collective implications of those themes, or its capacity to recall and reactivate family rules).

The issue of the symptomatic behavior being a link in a recursive interpersonal chain of symptom and maintenance, a key notion of a systemic viewpoint in family therapy, has been discussed extensively elsewhere (Sluzki, 1981).

The complementary idea of the value of the symptom as a rule-activator merits an additional comment. Symptoms are anchored in families when they accomplish the collective function of activators or reinforcers of specific collective rules. The example of a discussion becoming interrupted when one of the participants develops a headache, or that of an overall hostile climate switching to a caring mode when a family member—even one not actively involved in a hostile exchange—develops an asthma attack, shows clearly how the occurrence of a symptom has the function of overriding one set of interpersonal procedures in favor of another. Here it would suffice to notice that the child's symptom not only symbolizes and reminds everybody about the rule of silence, but even becomes an argument to *do more of the same,* that is, to reinforce the silence, on the basis of the argument that the symptom shows how sensitive and delicate the child is, and hence things should be kept from her. Chronic, rather stable symptoms contribute to retaining on a stable brain the family rules that they symbolize or activate. Such is the case of the symptom *elective mutism* in the families discussed above, which seems to fit quite tightly with the family-shared rules of silence, which, in turn, contribute to the retention of a mystified reality by not challenging its nature or validity.

According to which side of the argument one wishes to emphasize, it could be stated that the symptom reinforces the family rule, or that it denounces it. In fact, while the family functions in such a way as to maintain the symptom, it can be said to reinforce it. And when the therapist reorganizes the construction of the family's reality by means of, for instance, positively connoting the symptom, that procedure switches the value of the symptom to one of denunciation, as it advocates change in the direction of a reality in which the symptom does not have a reason for being.

Elective mutism, dramatic a symptom as it may be, constitutes just one of a vast number of language-related problems and symptoms—including so-called learning disabilities, school underachievement, and many other disturbances—that can be found with alarming frequency in bilingual families. These problems stagnate, become chronic, and seal the destiny of the identified patient and his family when dealt with following a route that includes intrapersonal labels, special educational programs, or, even more frequently, indifference. On the other hand, they respond readily to culturally sensitive, interactionally oriented interventions.

REFERENCES

Bateson, G., Jackson, D., Haley, J., & Weakland, J. Toward a theory of schizophrenia. *Behavioral Science*, 1956, *1*(4), 251-264.

Sluzki, C. Process of symptom production and patterns of symptom maintenance. *Journal of Marital Family Therapy*, 1981, *7*(3), 273-280.

Sluzki, C., & Veron, E. The double bind as universal pathogenic situation. *Family Process*, 1971, *10*(4), 397-410.

6. Assessment and Engagement Stages in Therapy with the Interracial Family

Jan Faulkner, MSW
Alameda County Mental Health Services
Oakland, California

George Kitahara Kich, PhD
Berkeley, California

THE COUPLE IN AN INTERRACIAL RELATIONSHIP AND THEIR INTERRA-
cial children often are expected to respond to the model of interventions and
services designed for families or couples who are alike racially. As a result,
the uniqueness of the interracial relationship may be minimized or viewed
from a pathological frame of reference. Therapy with interracial families
and couples presents special needs and considerations regardless of the race
or ethnic background of the therapist. Without an awareness of or sensitivity
to the complex dynamics of the multiracial family system, therapists may
inadvertently drive away their clients after the initial sessions. Over-
emphasis on race or ethnicity as determinants of the family's or couple's
problem is as detrimental to the therapy as underemphasizing or ignoring the
racial or ethnic dimensions. Values, beliefs, and stereotypes about ethnicity, race, and interracial marriage are important considerations in the
treatment process.

Ethnic and racial pluralism in America and increased interracial and
interethnic contact require a multiracial and multiethnic perspective on
family therapy (Giordano & Giordano, 1977). Earlier debates about the
therapy outcome of same-race or different-race therapists and clients (Bryson & Cody, 1973; Carkhuff & Pierce, 1967), though generally inconclu-
sive, have underscored the need for the therapist to be a more culturally
aware and sensitive person. The most recent writings have gone further:

- Focus on the essential salience and centrality of ethnic and racial factors
  in all family relations and therapy (Klein, 1977; McGoldrick, Pearce &
  Giordano, 1982)
- Analysis of the sociohistorical development of the values and norms of
  racial and ethnic groups (Carrillo, 1982; Jones & Korchin, 1982;
  Papajohn & Spiegel, 1975)
- Descriptions of the specific engagement and evaluation techniques in
  therapeutic work with a particular racial and ethnic family background
  (Bernal & Flores-Ortiz, 1982; Levine & Padilla, 1980).

These advances in the conceptualization of race and ethnicity are central
factors in therapy of all families. The frame of reference of the interracial
family has its own sociohistorical development and process.

Much of the literature on interracial relationships has focused on the
social and personal conflicts engendered by breaking community (and, until
1967, legal) restrictions on interracial marriage (Cheng & Yamamura, 1957;
Drake & Cayton, 1945; Golden, 1954). Issues of isolation from the commu-

nity (Simpson & Yinger, 1972), the need to conceal the marriage and its history from relatives or employers (Golden, 1954), the stability or instability of such marriages (Connor, 1976; DeVos, 1973; Gordon, 1964) and the psychodynamics of interracial relationships and sexuality (Fanon, 1967; Grier & Cobbs, 1968) have been discussed, often from a pessimistic perspective.

Generalizations about interracial relationships or interracial people have been made from the pathological to the normal, or from stereotypes to actual people. Stereotypes about race as well as myths of racial purity (Henriques, 1974) have contributed to a social view of interracial marriage as destructive, illicit, and unnatural. Only recently has empirical research focused on interracial relationships and interracial people from a positive, developmental, systems framework (Jacobs, 1977; Kich, 1982).

Jacobs (1977) found that:

> the decision to marry interracially and the marital process that follows generally resulted in a working through of racial feelings and beliefs leading to an openness in communication and interaction about racial matters, but not to a preoccupation with race. (pp. 192-193)

Communication about racial similarities and differences allows healthy resolutions of the generally difficult transitions in the family's life cycle (Kich, 1982). Often, the interracial couple and the interracial children must explore sensitive areas of the family's history and development in order to be able to accept and embrace the richness and complexity of their heritages. The family struggles to negotiate and work through areas of difference, both among themselves as family members and between themselves and other families. Racial and ethnic feelings, beliefs, and stereotypes intermingle with day-to-day relationship issues, like intimacy, money decisions, or child-rearing agreements.

The family therapist working with an interracial couple and their children must be sensitive and self-aware, especially in the beginning phases of treatment while gathering information about the family's life cycle as well as when incorporating the racial and ethnic dimensions within their problem-definition. This article will focus specifically on the initial contacts and interviews (the assessment and engagement processes) as the critical alliance-building and problem-formation stage in the therapy of interracial couples and families.

ASSESSMENT

Assessment and engagement processes occur simultaneously and are central to the initial stages of therapy with all families (Haley, 1973; McGoldrick et al., 1982; Minuchin, 1974). The therapist makes an assessment of the interracial family's strengths and weaknesses within at least the following areas:

- family life cycle
- intimacy and boundaries
- interracial children's response

Family Life Cycle

Transitions through the following expected developmental phases of the family (Glick & Kessler, 1980; Haley, 1973) have major implications for racial and ethnic themes: the beginning family (courtship, engagement, marriage); birth of first child; the sharing of influence with other authorities when the child enters school; the family with adolescents; the family as a launching center (the offsprings' separation from home and marriage); the family in its middle years; and the aging family (with return to single life at the death of a spouse).

Often, extended family support and acceptance is lost because of the selection of a different-race spouse. Each phase is affected by the response of the extended family to the marriage. As a result, interracial couples are often forced by their families or by social pressure to skip parts of each expected phase. Unresolved anger, hurt, and disappointment may contribute to family secrets, anniversary-related anxiety, or other family dysfunctions.

The family's responses to unexpected situational crises resulting from the loss of spouse or parent, illness or incapacitation, financial reversals, or role transitions by a family member (Glick & Kessler, 1980; Seward, 1972) may also provide clues to assessing dysfunctions. Although the parenting role may be inhibited due to the absence of a familial support base, many interracial couples we see often attempt to replace the loss of familial support by recreating a supportive family among other interracial couples. This type of networking also serves as a positive defensive gesture against the social and emotional isolation resulting from losses and social rejection.

Intimacy and Boundaries

Closeness and distance within the interracial family may be mediated by each family member's ability to accept and understand each other's differentness. Role enmeshment and submergence of racial and ethnic characteristics and heritages often result when the interracial couple experiences overwhelming negation, either from each other, from their extended families, or from society. The rigidity or flexibility of the family's rules, communication styles, and problem-solving methods must be assessed from a multiracial perspective by clarifying the family's level of comfort with itself as "different."

The family's rules or coping style (or its "blank," i.e., "the family that blanks together, stays together") in the face of negation can provide essential information about their strengths in maintaining intimacy and boundaries. What is the family's "blank?" How is the "blank" being reinforced, taught, or negated by the parents, parent, or one of the children? For instance, many interracial couples have collectively worked out a plan for dealing with the stares and curious looks they receive when out in public places. One couple prided themselves on quick answers when asked, "Are these your children?" Their responses, which ranged from, "Yes, notice how special each one was made?" to a blatant "Why?", reinforced their pride in their interracial family.

It is important for the therapist to be aware of the toll the mark of oppression can have on the interracial family and individual family members. In order to maintain its integrity and boundaries, the family and its members are pushed to defend themselves, either effectively or ineffectively. For example, one spouse may take on the speech, mannerisms and dress of the race of the partner who has remained in his or her community of origin. This defense is often attacked as being a submergence of one's racial heritage by being too much like the other. Other family members may defend individually in less overt ways, for instance, one partner will attempt to internalize the stress of the spouse experiencing the most overt forms of racism. This can become self-destructive behavior, for instance, one white wife was criticized severely for her "outlandish, overly revealing dress" by most of her white neighbors and, frequently, by her children. It became apparent through some successful family work that she was taking the pressure off her black spouse and interracial children by dressing in what she considered the "black dress" of the black women around her. Self-protectively, the spouse and children were using criticism and shame about her behavior as their family coping style ("blank") in their contacts with the black community. The family's mutual protectiveness had kept them from sharing their fears that the community would reject them for being an interracial family.

Protection processes, when used realistically and overtly as a means of creating intimacy and boundaries, are positive and reinforcing of the interracial family. However, when used in the service of enmeshment and submergence, mutual protection becomes a way of inhibiting communication and fostering racial and ethnic stereotypes.

Interracial Children's Responses

The interracial person, the child of the intermarriage, is not only the embodiment of the parents' racial differences, but is also an individual who must work through a very personal identity question (Hall, 1979; Jacobs, 1977; Kich, 1982). The family's unresolved racial and ethnic history and identity can be mirrored in their children's struggles with their exploration of parental heritages.

Interracial children are constantly asked, "*What* are you?" by others because their racial/ethnic heritage may not be clearly evident. They must develop a positive sense of self despite hearing stereotypes about "half-breeds," being mislabeled as belonging to other races or ethnicities, and having self-doubts about their racial labeling of themselves. The openness and comfort of each parent with the child's racial exploration, natural ambivalences, and questions can foster the identity resolution process. Information about the amount and quality of the child's intergenerational contact can provide important data about the family's strengths and cohesiveness.

Communication about differences between interracially married parents and their interracial child can be difficult despite positive intentions. For example, we asked a Eurasian teenage boy if his school friends had difficulty pronouncing his Japanese first name. His Jewish American father responded for him, saying that it was a beautiful name and no one would mispronounce it. The boy immediately responded that his friends not only mispronounced it, they made fun of it. The father continued talking, not hearing his son's refutation, and praised the Japanese meaning of the name. The father's intrusive negation of his son's experience prevented each of them from understanding and benefiting from the other.

Similar work with another family revealed that both parents were assuming a dual cultural/racial stance as a way of dealing effectively with their multiracial world and to enhance their parenting role with the children.

Outside the home the two parents used the cultural style of the other to create and maintain a place in the immediate community. The Chinese-American father used the straightforward and direct mannerisms of a white person to deal with the schools his children attended and then switched to his culture and tradition in the home. His white wife often made a similar switch during her weekly marketing treks to Chinatown. This couple's friends and relatives recognized their switches as positive and necessary. These same people were critical and rejecting when the couple's interracial children practiced switching. They considered it a form of "passing," which reflected their ambiguity about the children's racial identity. The parents rightfully defended their children's behavior, strengthening their multiracial identity development.

ENGAGEMENT

The therapist must develop an alliance with the interracial family that engages them in the problem-solving process. Successful engagement requires the therapist's use of self as an aware and sensitive person, open to the different frame of reference of the interracial family. The following techniques or concepts can facilitate the engagement/assessment process:

- self-disclosure and joining
- clarification about questions
- family self-identification
- hierarchy and culture

Self-Disclosure and Joining

As a way of joining the interracial family, the therapist may use self-disclosure to begin the process of exploring the family's presenting problem and history. The therapist may share not only personal experiences relevant to the particular family, but also experiences with other interracial families. For example, where appropriate, therapists may disclose their own personal involvement in an interracial family, their experience growing up in an ethnically or racially diverse neighborhood, or some other similarity with the family ("I'm also from a family with three boys and one girl").

Experience in working with other interracial families may be presented as a way of opening up the ethnic and racial dimensions of the family's history. For instance, the therapist might say, "Some of the interracial couples I work with have shared with me that they frequently must deal with other people's impolite stares. How do you two deal with that?'' Modeling of open communication about differences also extends to the therapist's lack of knowledge about a specific racial or ethnic group. Asking questions about the couple's cultural heritage allows the therapist to model a respectful and caring willingness to learn.

Clarifications about Questions

The therapist must clarify why developmental information is needed and why it is necessary to make racial or ethnic distinctions as the information is gathered. We often explain that we want to know them not only as a family, but also as a family that is unique. Differences are apparent at the first encounter with the family, and we make clear that we are acknowledging differences that often are not discussed easily or openly. We make the point that being different or holding different frames of reference can be mutually enriching when explored and accepted. Often, historical information (how the couple met, extended family's reactions to the marriage, etc.) is charged with previously unspoken emotional content that may be frightening and embarrassing to share, not only with the therapist but also with other family members.

The therapist will need to work at tempering any directive or intrusive approaches to questioning. For example, common questions such as, ''How did you meet?'' or ''Where did you meet?'' might carry an inference of societal laxity, that is, ''Who slipped up and allowed these two races to meet?'' The same questions asked of a family or couple of the same race may convey less charged judgments about class differences. However, the inter-racial family or couple may feel defensive or withdraw because they have been asked these questions so many times before under overtly critical or oppressive circumstances. We usually temper this question by asking, ''When did you meet?'', a question that often elicits a story answer. The therapist, comfortable enough to be respectfully silent, can allow the family to share what is comfortable for them. Often, if a family or couple is nervous, giving short and specific answers, for instance, ''We met in June 1970,'' we will encourage them by asking, ''Then what happened?''

Most families or couples are freed up to tell their story in their own way in a nonjudgmental setting. The accounts of meeting, courtship and marriage often contain vignettes about stresses and losses related to their mate selection, such as the need to respond to a racial slur directed at the couple or the relatives, the loss of extended family ties and friendships, and physical and economic changes in life style. The modeling of the process of clarification can provide the interracial family with a mutually respectful way of exploring emotionally charged areas of their experiences.

Family Self-Identification

The family's self-identification and self-description can present some of the most important clinical data for the therapist. The self-evaluative process inherent in working through differences and similarities, self- and other-perceptions, and differential social responses to the various family members is an active and at times paradoxical struggle for the interracial family. The therapist has the opportunity to assess ego and family intimacy strengths by asking the family how they label their interracial family. For instance, the therapist may ask, "Some of the interracial families I work with have asked me not to refer to them as mixed or inter-anything. How would you describe your family, and how do you want me to refer to you?" The submergence of one heritage or the other can be seen in the ways the family uses or develops a label or category for themselves. It can provide a clue about the degree of family resolution of possible issues of rejection, isolation, or loss due to their interracial life.

The family's use of humor and their awareness of racial stereotypes may be drawn out by the therapist during the discussion of self-labels. The family's resilience or rigidity to their own stereotypes about each other also can indicate areas of strength and difficulty. Clarification and self-disclosure by the therapist are ways of joining the family in its self-identification.

Hierarchy and Culture

The information gathering process should always reflect the therapist's recognition of the impact that racial differences have on parenting roles and styles (Sue, 1981). The therapist should begin the initial interview with the parents and seek their help concerning ways to include the children. A Hispanic father may expect to speak first, not only as a male (in his relationship with his wife) but also as an elder (in his relationship with his children). A black father may defer the beginning of the interview to his wife and reject the efforts of a child to begin the hour. In both examples the wife, if white, may not be as concerned about who begins the session. Similar sequences should be used when extended family members are present so as not to create conflict between kinship ties and hierarchical roles.

Therapists should be careful not to get caught in their own political righteousness about race and ethnicity. The focus should be on the family's experience of social or political oppression and their particular resolution of problems such as loss, conflicting parental styles and roles, or isolation. The therapist must consider openly the effects of racism on the self-concept of each spouse, whether a member of the majority society or of the minority society. How do they protect or support each other? Are they empathic or withdrawn? The choice of neighborhood can be indicative of the openness, submergence, or denial of both the spouses' heritages. The political stance of the spouses may be different from each other because of their own families' backgrounds. The interracial family's potential resolution of differences can be enhanced by the therapist's empathic exploration of each spouse's developmental and family history.

The roles of the members of an interracial family should be assessed in terms of their interaction in the decision-making process. How are the parents assuming their responsibilities around the roles of man/woman, mother/father, and husband/wife? What are the ethnic/racial effects associated with the roles? For instance, does the black mother use strict disciplining patterns because of her own childhood memories of the mothering role, or because she is frustrated about her ineffectiveness as a significant member of the interracial family? How are interpersonal relationships handled? What is the source of interpersonal reliance, self or family? How does the pattern of maintaining interpersonal relationships and reciprocity relate to the interracial mixture of the family? What effect does ethnicity or race have on the standards for right and wrong as practiced in the family? How is the parenting role enhanced and/or inhibited by the different cultural standards for right and wrong?

Loyalty dilemmas and attempts at resolving them are fundamental areas of conflict for interracial families. The interracial family members' choices will be affected by parental comfort about race and the extended family's openness and acceptance. Often, the loyalty dilemma is a reflection of a social or community conflict over acceptance or rejection of interracial marriage. The Asian American communities are particularly vocal and open about the debate, indicating the struggle over the loss of traditional Asian values and ritual (Kich, 1982).

Loyalty questions among family members can become a metaphor for other relationship problems experienced by the interracial family. Clarification and exploration by the therapist can bring into focus those aspects of the family's dilemma that can be resolved within the family and those which are manifestations of social or community struggles and stresses. Coping styles and problem-solving methods, drawn from the family's multiracial heritages, can be reframed with the family as cultural assets and tools rather than as dilemmas.

PROBLEM FORMATION

One of the therapist's tasks throughout the assessment and engagement stage has been to formulate problem statements that reflect the actual interaction of interracial dynamics and the communicational and structural processes of the family. Stereotypically, interracial relationships were understood as having been motivated by the spouses' unconscious needs to act out rebellious self-hatred and a form of identification with the aggressor. With this viewpoint, there could be no hope for a positive resolution for any of the interracial family's difficulties. In order to facilitate the family's restructuring and their resolution of presenting complaints, the therapist must incorporate interactional and social perspectives in the reframing process. Both perspectives potentially allow the immediate alleviation of the burden of guilt about the interracial marriage, allowing other dysfunctional family processes to be assessed. Family strengths and richness can also be tapped. Finally, involving the family members in selecting the target problems and in setting clear potentially realizable goals brings together both the assessment and the engagement processes with the family.

CONCLUSIONS

Because interracial families are so diverse in their racial and ethnic combinations, generalizations about therapy must be made cautiously. However, the assessment and engagement processes previously outlined can provide useful rules of thumb for the therapist in determining how the family's interracial life detracts from or fosters positive and enhancing communication and boundary maintenance.

The therapist's use of self throughout the therapy with interracial families and children necessitates personal clarity about race and ethnicity, especially in terms of family of origin. Sensitivity and openness to the interracial family can develop as a result of the therapist's self-valuation of racial and ethnic heritages.

In summary, the question may be asked, does the therapist have to be deeply knowledgeable about each ethnic/racial group in order to be effective with the interracial family? The answer of course is no, but it is important for the therapist:

- to be open to being educated by the family about ethnic/racial contents (traditions, styles, etc.)
- to be able to tolerate making mistakes in interpretations, and even more importantly, able to work through misinterpretations with the family, as a model for the way the family could work through their misinterpretations
- to be sensitive to social and personal judgments and stereotypes about interracial relationships
- to understand efforts to resolve the problem: How has this interracial family approached and worked through expected and unexpected developmental phases of family life?
- to be self-aware and to value personal ethnic/racial roots and heritage.

REFERENCES

Bernal, G., & Flores-Ortiz, Y. Latino families in therapy: Engagement and evaluation. *Journal of Marital and Family Therapy,* July 1982, 357-365.

Bryson, S., & Cody, J. Relationship of race and level of understanding between counselor and client. *Journal of Counseling Psychology,* 1973, *20,* 495-498.

Carkhuff, R., & Pierce, R. Differential effects of therapist race and social class upon patient depth of self-exploration in the initial clinical interview. *Journal of Counseling Psychology,* 1967, *31,* 632-634.

Carrillo, C. Changing norms of Hispanic families: Implications for treatment. In E. Jones & S. Korchin (Eds.), *Minority Mental Health.* New York: Holt, Rinehart & Winston, 1982.

Cheng, C., & Yamamura, D. Interracial marriage and divorce in Hawaii. *Social Forces,* 1957, *36,* 77-84.

Connor, J. *A study of the marital stability of Japanese war brides.* San Francisco: R. & E. Associates, 1976.

DeVos, G. Personality patterns and problems of adjustment in American-Japanese intercultural marriages. *Asian Folklore and Social Life Monographs,* 1973, *49.*

Drake, S., & Cayton, H. *Black metropolis.* New York: Harcourt, Brace, 1945.

Fanon, R. *Black skin, white masks.* New York: Grove Press, 1967.

Giordano, J., & Giordano, G. *The ethno-cultural factor in mental health: A literature review and bibliography.* New York: Institute on Pluralism and Group Identity of the American Jewish Committee, 1977.

Glick, J., & Kessler, D. Marital and family therapy. New York: Grune & Stratton, 1980.

Golden, J. Patterns of Negro-white intermarriage. *American Sociological Review,* 1954, *19,* 144-166.

Gordon, A. *Intermarriage: Interfaith, interracial, interethnic.* Boston: Beacon Press, 1964.

Grier, W., & Cobbs, P. *Black rage.* New York: Basic Books, 1968.

Haley, J. *Uncommon therapy.* New York: Norton, 1973.

Hall, C. *Ethnic identity of racially mixed people: A study of Black-Japanese.* Unpublished doctoral dissertation, University of California, Los Angeles, 1979.

Henriques, F. *Children of Caliban.* London: Martin Secker & Warburg, 1974.

Jacobs, J. *Black/white interracial families: Marital process and identity development in young children.* Unpublished doctoral dissertation, Wright Institute, Berkeley, Calif., 1977.

Jones, E. Effects of race on psychotherapy process and outcome. *Psychotherapy: Theory, Research & Practice,* 1978, *15,* 226-236.

Jones, E., & Korchin, S. (Eds.). *Minority mental health.* New York: Holt, Rinehart & Winston, 1982.

Kich, G. *Eurasians: Ethnic/racial identity development of biracial Japanese/white adults.* Unpublished doctoral dissertation, Wright Institute, Berkeley, Calif., 1982.

Klein, J. *Jewish identity and self-esteem.* Unpublished doctoral dissertation, Wright Institute, Berkeley, Calif., 1977.

LeVine, E., & Padilla, A. *Crossing cultures in therapy: Pluralistic counseling for the Hispanic.* Monterey, Calif.: Brooks/Cole, 1980.

McGoldrick, M., Pearce, J., & Giordano, J. *Ethnicity and family therapy.* New York: Guilford Press, 1982.

Minuchin, S. *Families and family therapy.* Cambridge, Mass.: Harvard University Press, 1974.

Papajohn, J., & Spiegel, J. *Transactions in families: A modern approach for resolving cultural and generational conflicts.* San Francisco: Jossey-Bass, 1975.

Seward, G. *Psychotherapy and culture conflict in community mental health* (2nd ed.). New York: Ronald Press, 1972.

Simpson, G., & Yinger, J. *Racial and cultural minorities: An analysis of prejudice and discrimination* (4th ed.). New York: Harper & Row, 1972.

Sue, D. *Counseling the culturally different: Theory and practice.* New York: John Wiley, 1981.

7. International Trade in Family Therapy: Parallels between Societal and Therapeutic Values

Douglas Breunlin, MSSA
Family Systems Program
Institute for Juvenile Research
Chicago, Illinois

Max Cornwell, BA, BSocStud (Hns)
School of Social Work
University of New South Wales
Sydney, Australia

The Family Therapy Institute of Australia
Sydney, Australia

Brian Cade, CSW, BA
The Family Institute
Cardiff, Wales, U.K.

The authors wish to thank Dick Schwartz, Betty Karrer, Kathy Stathos, Marty Bennett, and Hilary Buzas for their support and comments that helped to strengthen this article.

As the decade of the eighties unfolds, two interrelated trends have begun to play a significant role in the development of the field of family therapy. The first is the dramatic emergence of family therapy as a recognized international movement with new and important contributions being made and shared among family therapists throughout the world. The movement is characterized by a flourishing of journals and conferences with an international flavor, and appearances of experts who travel to foreign countries to present their work. The community of family therapists now spans the globe. The second trend is the growing recognition of culture as a significant variable influencing the conceptual and practical base of family therapy. This emphasis on culture has focused primarily upon the issue of ethnicity; consequently, a rich literature is emerging that defines how therapy must be adjusted to accommodate the ethnic values of the many subcultures that make up heterogeneous societies such as the United States or Australia (McGoldrick, Pearce, & Giordano, 1982). We believe a similar process of accommodation takes place at a societal level; that is, the values that govern a model of family therapy are, to some extent, similar to some of the prevalent values of the country in which the model developed. As international trade in family therapy ideas expands in the eighties, we believe the world community of family therapists can profit from a close examination of how family therapies develop within a given country, and of how they must be adapted when they are imported by other countries.

We will begin this examination by identifying some of the prevalent values of the communication approach of family therapy (Madanes & Haley, 1977), and will attempt to show how these values resonate with some prevalent societal values in the United States, the country in which the approach was developed. We will then identify some prevalent societal values in Britain and Australia, two countries that have imported and used this approach extensively; and suggest how the therapy associated with it may require modification to achieve resonance with the values of these importing countries. Such a process of accommodation is inevitable, but it is often ignored or denied both by the exporters and importers of a therapy. Family therapists who are aware of this process, regardless of the approach to therapy they use, will be better able to declare and incorporate into their discussions the societal underpinnings of their therapies.

Several factors influenced our decision to select the United States as the exporting country and Britain and Australia as the importing countries. First, as therapists and teachers, we are most familiar with the communication approach developed in the United States. Second, we worked together extensively in Britain at the Family Institute in Cardiff (Breunlin was a staff member 1975-78; Cornwell was a visiting therapist 1977-78; Cade has been a staff member 1973-present). Finally, we have each visited and taught in all three countries, and are familiar with the development of family therapy in the country in which each of us now works.

By designating the United States as the exporting country, we are not suggesting that it is the only, or even the primary, exporter of therapies (psychoanalysis and Jungian analysis come from Europe). Had we possessed the requisite background, we could, for instance, have designated Italy as the exporting country and examined the accommodation essential in importing the Milan approach into any of the countries where it is now being used.

It is possible to discuss this process of accommodation within the scope of this article only if we simplify our presentations of societal values in a way that constitutes a partial reality, bordering upon cultural stereotyping, of all three countries. We hope to identify predominant values that transcend the multicultural makeup of each of the three countries, while at the same time acknowledging that even these values, to some extent, are in a state of flux. For example, our discussion of Australia totally ignores aboriginal societies, subtle class variables, and the impact of postwar immigration and internationalism. Where possible, we will use idioms to capture these predominant values because they are succinct and capture the flavor of the society.

Our approach is comparative, in the sense that the values of each country are presented in relation to the other two. For instance, we consider the United States to value change more than Britain, with Australia falling somewhere between the two.

Family therapy fields in the three countries are influenced somewhat by the societal contexts in which they operate. These contexts influence both how therapies are developed and imported. In the United States, for instance, the field of family therapy is highly competitive, a phenomenon that parallels the nature of the marketplace there. Models of therapy are consumer products, and to market their products the proponents of the many models stress their respective advantages (Liddle, 1982). This creates a context in which differences rather than similarities in models are stressed, and in which mental health professionals are encouraged to declare an allegiance to a particular model. In Britain, health care has been nationalized, thus removing it from the marketplace and making it less susceptible to consumerism and competition. Family therapy, therefore, is not a private sector consumer product and the marketing aspect of the models, including the emphasis upon differences and conceptual and practical purity, is far less noticeable. Consequently, the family therapy field in

Britain is more receptive to eclecticism and integration (Cooklyn, 1978; Skynner, 1980). A context is readily available, therefore, to import and use aspects of therapies from other countries. In Australia, as in Britain, therapy is centered on the public rather than the private sector. Also, as an immigrant society, Australia has relied heavily upon the importation of ideas. The field of family therapy in Australia follows this pattern, but not without some ambivalence regarding the appropriateness of such endeavors (Cornwell, 1982; Stagoll, 1983). The British and Australian reliance on public sector activity also has a marked impact on the distribution and career structures of therapists. One is much less likely to find practitioners who regard themselves exclusively as family therapists— family therapy tends to be regarded as a modality to link with a variety of social interventions.

VALUES OF THE COMMUNICATION APPROACH

The term *communication approach* was used by Madanes and Haley (1977) to refer to those family therapies that derived specifically from cybernetics and systems theory, as opposed to those that originally had roots in individual therapies such as psychoanalysis, behavioral, or gestalt. The family therapy models subsumed under this approach are the structural (Minuchin, 1974; Minuchin & Fishman, 1981; Minuchin, Montalvo, Guerney, Rosman & Shumer 1967) and the various strategic models; the Mental Research Institute (MRI) (Fisch, Weakland and Segal, 1981; Watzlawick, Weakland & Fisch, 1974), the strategic therapy of Haley (1973, 1976, 1980), Madanes (1981) and the Ackerman brief therapy group (Papp, 1980). Although these models originated at different centers and involved different innovators and treatment populations, they share several values, some of them overt and others that may be inferred from observing the procedures of the models (Stanton, 1981).

The communication approach ascribes problem behavior to the current interactional context in which it occurs. Hence, the approach places particular value upon interactional processes occurring in the present, and little attention is given to history. Developed from work with severe problems such as schizophrenia (Bateson, Jackson, Haley & Weakland, 1956) and chronic delinquency (Minuchin et al., 1967), the approach, as it evolved, became change oriented and optimistic, largely because successful efforts to change the interactional context did resolve the problems.

The models subsumed under the approach share several procedures for altering the interactional context of a problem. The first is the setting of clear goals, which are then pursued methodically with a view toward achieving a change in context that will bring about a satisfactory outcome. The second is the creation of a strong therapeutic system in which the therapist joins the family and functions as an expert by establishing a central and active position. Third, the therapy is pragmatic with interventions selected on the basis of their ability to change the context. Fourth, the approach operates swiftly, with attempts at change occurring within the first few sessions; and finally, it is brief (generally less than ten sessions). In summary, the communication approach places particular value upon all of the following: change, optimism, process, goals and outcome, planning, pragmatism, joining, action, expertise, swiftness, and brevity.

The various models subsumed under the communication approach vary in how these values are operationalized. These distinctions are important in understanding how the approach is adapted for use in Britain and Australia. The approach recognizes that in any interactional context problems are both system-maintained and system-maintaining (Minuchin & Fishman, 1981). One can, therefore, produce change either by altering the nature of the system or by changing the stabilizing or protective function of the problem. If the former method is chosen, then efforts are directed toward reorganizing or restructuring the family, and goals are defined accordingly (Haley, 1980; Minuchin & Fishman, 1981). If the latter method is selected, then the goals are more problem oriented (Madanes, 1981; Watzlawick et al., 1974).

Another distinction is the degree to which the therapist changes interactional processes occurring within a session rather than changing them between sessions. When focusing upon processes within a session, action takes the form of an enactment: the acting out of behavioral scenarios under the guidance, but not necessarily the participation, of the therapist (Haley, 1980; Madanes, 1981; Minuchin & Fishman, 1981). When between session processes are targeted, carefully planned directives are used to specify how the family is to act after they leave the session (Haley, 1976; Madanes, 1981; Watzlawick et al., 1974).

The therapist must also decide whether to be very direct in requesting a change in process, or to be more indirect. If a direct approach is used, the therapist is likely to challenge the family in a supportive way to experience itself differently (Minuchin & Fishman, 1981). To overcome the family's tendency to prefer existing patterns of interaction, the therapist creates sufficient intensity in the enactment to trigger new responses (Minuchin & Fishman, 1981). If the therapist works indirectly, then the interventions tend to be paradoxical in the sense that the family is encouraged to remain the same in such a way that they can no longer continue behaving in the same way (Haley, 1976; Madanes, 1981; Watzlawick et al., 1974).

The type of relationship the therapist establishes with the family will also vary. The therapist may enter the family and form strong relationships with its members in a way that requires considerable use of self and high levels of proximity (Haley, 1980; Minuchin, 1974; Minuchin & Fishman, 1981). Or the relationship may be established through a careful understanding and use of the family's language (Fisch et al., 1981; Watzlawick et al., 1974).

At one level, the particular interventions and therapist styles of the various models appear quite different. At another level, however, they only represent different ways of operationalizing the same values. Experienced therapists integrate those aspects of the models which are syntonic with their personal style. Similarly, when a communication approach is adopted for use in a particular country, these same values must be modified and operationalized in ways that provide a functional fit between therapy and society.

THE COMMUNICATION APPROACH AND VALUES IN THE UNITED STATES

Although the United States is a multicultural and complex society, there are some values associated with an advanced technological and post-industrial society that could be said to constitute the dominant contemporary ethos. These values can be related to parallel values in the communication approach.

Papajohn and Spiegel (1975) contrasted dominant trends between middle class American and Puerto Rican working class value orientations with respect to five modalities: time, activity, man-nature, relational and nature of man. They argued that Americans emphasize the future more than the present and the present more than the past. This emphasis is related to the value that Americans place on progress; the never ending quest for improvement, whether economic, technological or social. To achieve this progress, Americans accept a society which is always changing. Obsolete buildings are demolished and replaced with more modern structures. Houses, cars, and other products are changed regularly. The status quo does not last for long.

With respect to activity, Americans prefer doing over being. They are goal oriented, planning for and expecting success in their endeavors. They place a high value on action. The United States is very much a "don't just sit there, do something" society in which "action speaks louder than words." All areas of living from work to recreation are permeated by high levels of activity. The United States is also a country in a hurry where decisions are made and action taken quickly. This "don't leave till tomorrow what can be done today" value carries an element of *risk* which most Americans are prepared to accept. To the British and Australians, Americans often appear naive because they do make decisions quickly, basing their decisions on a succinct and selective gathering and analysis of information pertinent to those decisions.

Progress is achieved through a continued mastery of every aspect of nature through the application of an ever more sophisticated technology. The country's success in this endeavor has produced a sense of optimism with respect to outcome; if a situation is not satisfactory, it can be made better. Americans are also favorably disposed toward experts. Experts are viewed as individuals who, having mastered a friendly technology, are committed to using that technology to solve problems, whether medical, legal, scientific, political, or social.

In the relational modality, individuality is valued above collaterality or lineality. This value orientation probably accounts for the popularity of individual therapies, which have been challenged only recently through the introduction of systems theory and cybernetics into the mental health professions. Finally, the view of man as neutral or mixed rather than solely good or evil implies that bad or mad behavior can be changed.

All of these values are reflected in interpersonal relationships. Compared with the British, Americans are perceived more readily as a friendly and open people. When strangers meet, intimate details of their respective backgrounds are exchanged immediately. Relationships develop quickly, and people will report that they feel comfortable with and know one another well having met only a short while ago. This openness allows for a high degree of proximity characterized by fairly open displays of affect both publicly and privately. Americans are also prepared to take risks to alter relationships, using their openness as a vehicle to process and resolve relationships problems.

An American family taking part in a communication approach to family therapy in the United States would, therefore, not be surprised to hear the therapist talk about change, and describe change in terms of the resolution of problems. In most cases, the family would accept the therapist's optimism about a favorable outcome and would readily accept the idea that the outcome could be achieved quickly through an application of the therapist's careful planning and technical expertise. The family would accept a plan based upon limited information gathered in the first few sessions. They would trust the therapist and be prepared to accept a risk by taking action to solve the problem, either in the session in the form of an enactment or between sessions as part of a directive. Although a family might initially object, in most cases it would be possible to activate key relationships, and to request and obtain a restating of those relationships either with some intensity in the session or through a directive between sessions.

American television constitutes a metaphor for the similarities between the values of American society and those that govern a communication approach to a family therapy session. In the typical American TV show, a central character, or characters, is confronted by a dilemma that must be resolved within the time frame of an hour or half-hour program. Relatively little emphasis is given to background information or to the development of characters. Relationships between characters unfold rapidly and little attention is given to details of plot. Dialogue is generally superficial and often serves only to provide information or to punctuate scenes that are filled with action. The program builds momentum quickly until the deciding scene, in which the principal characters take some decisive action to solve the dilemma. The action is usually very intense with high levels of conflict or emotions expressed openly. In the deciding scene, not only is the dilemma resolved, but little or no ambiguity concerning outcome is left to the audience. In most situations some sort of change—usually for the better—has taken place.

IMPORTING A COMMUNICATION APPROACH INTO BRITAIN

The prevalence of the communication approach in articles in the British family therapy literature and the growing number of centers practicing these models attest to its popularity in Britain. An examination of some selected British values, however, suggests that the accommodation of these models with British society would be problematic were it to be imported and practiced as in the United States. We will examine those values that pose a problem, and suggest how certain modifications are being made to assist the process of accommodation.

Perhaps the greatest incongruity with British values is the position regarding change. Given the dialectic of change versus permanence, the British prefer the latter. Steeped as the British are in hundreds of years of tradition, it is not surprising that they are cautious about change. Change can mean undoing rather than progress, and that undoing may make a situation worse rather than better. The British are also less willing to apply technology to solve social problems (at a societal, family, and individual level), believing that some social problems are not amenable to technical solutions. They also prefer to understand all of the complexities of a problem prior to making any decision; hence, risks are not taken as readily, and decisions are made more slowly. Since they are without ready-made technical expertise and are cognizant of the enormous complexity of all social systems, it is not surprising that the British are also somewhat pessimistic about the outcome of any effort to solve a social problem. The notion of "muddling through" gradually, while canvassing possible consequences, enjoys widespread favor.

Where Americans prefer action, the British prefer language as the modus operandi of social relationships. The American use of English is characterized by volubility, slang, and technicality, while the English emphasize range of vocabulary and a feel for precision and nuance that to Americans may appear formal and even pedantic.

The conduct of interpersonal relationships in Britain is also quite different. One major feature is the existence of a class system that greatly restricts social mobility. When strangers meet, a mutual reserve exists, and few intimate details are exchanged. A relationship develops over time, perhaps years, and even then many details of one's life may not be shared. The American tendency to "let it all hang out" and to form personal relationships quickly often is regarded by the British as a sign of superficiality, transience, and egotism, and even as a breach of etiquette. The British value "keeping oneself to oneself." When a problem exists, it should be handled within the family, as it is important "not to wash one's dirty laundry in public."

The British are far less direct about their interpersonal relationships, seldom making direct statements about how they function or how they wish them to be different. They maintain a "proper" distance when relating, and avoid strong displays of affect. The typical British television program serves as a metaphor for British values, and suggests how these values are in many ways quite dissimilar to the values of a communication approach to family therapy. Like American TV, a British program generally places a central character or characters in some dilemma, but that dilemma is not necessarily resolved by the conclusion of the program. Instead, the many facets of the dilemma are explored, and the viewer is frequently left with little or no movement having occurred. In place of action one often finds dialogue, with extensive conversations probing the subtleties of relationships, enhancing rather than resolving the complexities of the dilemma. Viewers of British TV are often left without clear-cut outcomes and must often tolerate high levels of ambiguity. Frequently, the process is more important than the outcome, perhaps reflecting the British belief that it is more important to follow the rules than to win the game.

In contrast to American TV's tendency to simplify emotions and to put them openly on display, British TV is much more likely to focus on the complexities of emotional states but to underplay the expression of emotion, reflecting the British tendency to be embarrassed by or disapproving of public displays of feelings. The "stiff upper lip" remains for many the proper attitude in moments of either joy or distress. The British playwright Alan Bennett has observed, "They are the most embarrassed people in the world. They cannot look each other in the face . . ."

We believe that British therapists, influenced as they are by their own societal values, have adjusted the models of the communication approach to fit their society. For instance, from the outset of therapy they are likely to move more slowly, conducting more extensive assessments, and taking more time to form relationships with families. Their careful use of language helps define the etiquette of the relationship, and instead of reaching a simple formulation of the problem, they explore complexities in detail before moving ahead. Emphasis is placed on talking about the problem, rather than moving rapidly into an enactment. They lead the discussion carefully to enhance joining, conveying an attitude of proficient and respectful interest. Judicious care is taken not to imply premature familiarity. The therapist avoids the suggestion that therapy may provoke rapid or extensive change; rather, the family difficulty is regarded as probably manageable over time, provided the "right" amount of data is accumulated and analyzed. The therapist reassures the family that change should not imply "throwing out the baby with the bathwater," that is, unwittingly removing qualities of life valued by the family, or creating new problems by oversimple formulations and hasty action. The therapist is cautious and responsible, while the family is polite and willing to exercise discretion privately in how much value to accord to therapy. The family may agree to complete a task between sessions and then not do so. Neither therapist nor family would openly express negative views of the task or the relationship, but would proceed to consider more data before designing a new task. This in turn might or might not be completed, depending (publicly) on whether the "correct data" had been surmised. Levels of intensity are adroitly monitored, because of the societal emphasis on avoiding undue proximity, affect-laden revelations, or statements that directly define or redefine relationships. Therapy sessions in Britain are less likely to draw on enactment; where enactment and other intensity inducing modes are employed, a corresponding emphasis is placed on joining, preparation, and review, to ensure that a family does not experience a breach of its decorum, integrity, and safety.

Considerable reliance is placed on indirect interventions, often with the therapist adopting a one-down position, with subtle nuances in language to finely respond to mood levels and shifts in proximity. Through the use of positive connotation and reframing, the therapist can support permanence, while fostering change paradoxically through a prescription of the system or symptom (Breunlin & Cade, 1981; Cade, 1980). Where more direct interventions are chosen, patience and time are necessary, because of the demand to use accumulations of less affective, verbal procedures in preference to physical maneuvers. Interestingly, little is known about how the class system affects social definitions of "expert."

IMPORTING A COMMUNICATION APPROACH INTO AUSTRALIA

It is not easy to describe Australian culture, because western settlement is relatively late. The British and Irish foundations of non-aboriginal Australia are tempered by periodic groundswells of emergent nationalism and the rapidly growing impact of links with the United States, along with increasing recognition of Australia's context in Asia and the Pacific. This is further complicated by a massive influx of postwar immigrations. Australia is an immigrant culture that relies heavily on importing ideas and applying them to the unusual sociogeographic setting—a nation of improvisers who are suspicious of intellectualism and theoretical "purity." The ongoing dialectic between foreign and local values is a predominant characteristic of the society, with profoundly complex alliances and divisions. Australian society is extremely conflicted in its response to other cultures, appearing simultaneously to welcome foreign expertise and approval and to denigrate local endeavor, while being resentful of the implied inferiority and seeking arenas to redress the perceived imbalance. This is especially significant given the cultural ethos of egalitarianism, which finds particularly strong expression in a posture of ironic, mordant humor as a means of social leveling. It is as if the Australian lives predominantly "meta" to the culture, ridiculing both himself and others for taking life seriously.

Australians are ambivalent about change. The social emphasis on materialism is to some degree countered by an underlying pessimism, traditionally linked with earlier difficulties in accommodating to an alien and seemingly hostile environment, and the experience of convict and colonial administrations. The tinge of fatalism in the society is seen as counteracting the competitiveness and self-importance associated with the American view of change. Americans are typically portrayed as having too much money, and as being opinionated, naive, and "too smooth," not taking life squarely on the chin but shouldering uncomfortable realities aside, while the English are held to be distant, formal, inflexible and unjustifiably condescending, as they would be unable to contend with the harsh demands of the landscape without a servant class. For an Australian, any hint of self-importance or pretentiousness may invite ridicule. One supposedly demonstrates capacity by action rather than words or outward displays of superiority. Irrespective of wealth, status, or education, the cultural ideal is an attitude of self-deprecating informality and egalitarianism. Australians are likely to accept the possibility of small increments of change rather than dramatic shifts, and considerable value is placed on the role of "battler," the little everyman figure who "has a go" against perverse odds, while keeping himself in insignificant perspective. The gesture is all, because in the end one is flying in the face of an uncaring universe: The weather or fate or some "bastard" will get you in the end, so you may as well be brave, "have a laugh," "take it on the chin" and be a "good bloke," a person who is unpretentious, courageous and loyal.

Being a "good bloke," particularly for men, is very important. It defines a style of relating which involves ample portions of gregariousness and self-deprecation. People in authority, who are pretentious or have the power to harm you, should be viewed with suspicion unless they are demonstrably "good blokes." To qualify as a "good bloke," people in authority must be competent, prepared to "have a go," but must not take the role or themselves too seriously.

At an interpersonal level, while Australians are quite informal, they maintain emotional distance. Good neighbors are those who mind their own business and keep to their backyards. It is very important not to be intrusive. If someone is upset, it is often not appropriate to approach unless the person signals a desire for this. To intrude or encourage self-revelation is to exploit vulnerability, to take advantage of someone while they are down. Remaining apart shows respect for others while they regain composure. Privacy, then, is also very important. Neighbors and outsiders do not invade the privacy of others, and parents do not invade the privacy of older children, fearing that if they intrude they may drive the child away and only make any problem worse. Public displays of emotion are avoided, as they are thought to make others uncomfortable and to betray egocentrism, vulnerability, self-pity, or mawkishness. Sentiment outside the family is often expressed indirectly, and through specific institutions such as "mateship."

In Australia, sex roles were historically very rigidly defined, with men acting more instrumentally and women being more expressive. Many institutional legacies of this pattern linger, despite increasing opposition, affecting general societal trends. This, in turn, has an effect on therapists' occupational choices, career patterns, and even, perhaps, their preferred modes of interventions (Cornwell, 1982; Topham, 1982).

Australian television can be seen as a metaphor for the society, but in a less obvious way than we have suggested for the United States and Britain. Much television is imported from both countries, and ever increasingly from Europe and Asia, paralleling the trend toward importing in the society at large. The homemade product emphasizes sports, quiz shows, and soap operas in which the dominant popular values are given full encouragement, along with an emerging, more "high minded," nationalist focus on documentaries and "art" films. In TV dramas, "baddies" are often authorities or snobs. Sometimes the heroes win, but if they lose, they retain their decency, and may recover to fight another day. Wrongs may one day be redressed. There is considerable emphasis on informality, friendliness, physical bravery, unscholastic intelligence—an anti-sophistication motif. Women's roles tend to display a narrow repertoire of stereotypes. Australians proclaim their film-making, but worry about whether it's good enough to overcome American and British "prejudice" against them.

The above discussion suggests to us that in practicing a communication approach in Australia, the following modifications should be made. The therapist must be prepared not to be viewed by the family as a benevolent expert. Although the family will tend to relate quite informally from the outset, meaningful joining will not occur until the therapist is regarded as authentic. The joining phase is characterized by unintrusive informality, often using casual humor, while overtly and covertly emphasizing privacy and respect for social distance on significant matters. Extra work by the therapist may be required to involve males in domains once defined as exclusively female. If the therapist can relate more instrumentally to males and more expressively to females, some pitfalls can be avoided, at least in early stages when less individualized responses are usually necessary. Australians will "play" at a stereotype while gauging context. The therapist will tend not to make direct requests that invite too much proximity or open displays of emotion, without at least considering mutual options to permit face-saving. Family therapists in Australia are divided about the degree to which emotional intensity and enactment are valued. At one end of the continuum are those who link the intensity of enactment with analytically-based catharsis; at the other are those who prefer the less overt, perhaps less personally involving means of influence of the strategic models. Regrettably, therapists until recently have not always been open to taking a more rigorous look at common societal mores, but may rather reflect therapist subcultures within the broader complex of competing values. Similar confusion pervades the notion of hierarchy, with some therapists adopting a more doctrinaire view, and others asserting that Australian parents value a more flexible position on hierarchy, in keeping with egalitarian themes. Certainly, many Australian parents seem reluctant to "intrude" on the concerns and behavior of older children, for fear of losing affection and driving them away by breaching norms of privacy. But the reality is that Australian society now encompasses a vast range of preferred family modes that may invite differential response on subcultural as well as cultural norms. Public shifts of social policy from assimilation of immigrant cultures to multi-culturalism both reflect and guide such dilemmas.

For traditional Australian culture, with which we have largely been concerned, the strategic models have a resonance of values. One area where the fit is quite good is pragmatism. Australian therapists and families would react favorably to a therapy which uses ingenuity to create solutions that uniquely fit specific problems. The one-down style can help them to be seen as "good blokes." The gentle art of reframing allows the therapist access to relationship issues without appearing to be intrusive, and, as with the British, the model does not require undue proximity or open displays of emotion. Paradox often fits while "playing" at one level, while "knowing" at another.

In summary, the valued therapist is competent, pragmatic, calm, sincere, modest, informal, friendly, cautiously optimistic, unintrusive, unacademic and preferably humorous. The Australian family will laugh and tell you that's a tall order, so don't get smart with us. "Therapy " is Anglo-American, mate: What sort of Australian are you?

DISCUSSION

In the above discussion, we are aware that we have taken great license to generalize with respect to societal values in the United States, Britain, and Australia. Again, we are presenting a metaphor of a process: the inevitable accommodation that occurs between therapeutic and societal values. Our observations about this process are based on our shared clinical experience with hundreds of families treated or observed in all three countries. In Britain, we worked together to adapt the communication approach to British families, experiencing what worked and what did not. In America, while watching Breunlin work, Cornwell and Cade would often remark: "We could never get away with that at home" (Australia or Britain). A similiar process occurred with Breunlin and Cade in Australia. We are fortunate to have shared these cross-cultural experiences, recognizing that by stepping outside our respective societal frames of reference, we are more able to identify some of the values underpinning these frames.

Still, in all of this, we are presenting the experiences of three individuals who, separately and together, bring inevitable biases to the data. We are hopeful that readers of this article, bringing as they do inherent expertise to an understanding of their own society, will enhance this discussion by providing feedback to these ideas and adding their own.

In this discussion we have focused upon the process of accommodation between therapeutic and societal values. At another level, however, a therapy inevitably challenges those values that in some way inhibit change. For instance, family therapy challenges the value of individuality by replacing the linearity of this value with a value for interconnectedness. This dialectic between values that challenge and values that accommodate is very subtle and finely balanced. For instance, assertiveness training builds upon the American values of openness, directness, and personal autonomy while challenging values of excessive politeness and extreme altruism. For a therapy to be effective, it must produce some degree of pattern dislocation, but not so much as to be rejected outright by the system (Montalvo, 1973). Minuchin and Fishman (1981) stressed the need for therapists to be able to violate socially acceptable ways of relating in order to penetrate a family and activate it to experience new transactions. This violation may include disagreeing with family members or siding with one over another; in short, being unfair. In the United States, such a violation of socially acceptable ways of relating may be possible because it produces a tolerable level of pattern dislocation. In Britain, on the other hand, where the value of fairness is very strong, taking sides overtly may cause too great a pattern dislocation, which a British family would be unable to tolerate. We believe the process of accommodation we have described will modify interventions to circumvent excessive pattern dislocation, but this process raises the question: Is it possible for the process of accommodation to so modify an intervention as to make it ineffective? For instance, if in Britain certain structural interventions are modified to make them less direct and intense, will these interventions still carry the desired impact?

We should also note that an American therapist successfully demonstrating a communication approach to family therapy in Britain does not represent evidence that the model translates easily. An American therapist is not governed by British values and so may unwittingly violate those values. However, the family will see the American therapist as an outsider and will, therefore, tolerate such violations.

In fact, demonstration interviews of family therapy by visiting experts working with British or Australian families are often just as dramatic as anything one might see in America, but this does not mean that a British therapist and British family can so easily violate the societal values that govern both.

We believe there is a growing need to answer these as well as related questions about the use of family therapy models within a given country. The international dialogue should continue and include the following ground rules. First, the country that develops a therapy, that is, the exporting country, should articulate the societal values that underpin the therapy. Second, the country that adopts the model, the importing country, should examine the societal values that will modify the therapy. Third, a critical analysis of the family therapy concepts and practices that are effective in a given country should be undertaken. Fourth, the language of the international movement must be better defined. For example, to refer to structural or strategic family therapy in Britain, Australia, and America as the same phenomenon may be inaccurate. Just as Eskimos have many names for snow, so we may require more names for the practice of a particular school of family therapy. Finally, and perhaps most important, it is vital that the family therapy community of each country recognize the uniqueness and value of its contribution both for its own country and for the world community. When all of this occurs a truly international dialogue will begin.

REFERENCES

Bateson, G., Jackson, D., Haley, J. & Weakland, J. Toward a theory of schizophrenia. *Behavioral Science*, 1956, *1*, 251-64.

Breunlin, D.C., & Cade, B.W. Intervening in family systems with observer messages. *Journal of Marital and Family Therapy*, 1981, *7*, 453-460.

Cade, B.W. Strategic therapy. *Journal of Family Therapy*, 1980, *2*, 89-99.

Cade, B.W. The potency of impotence. *The Australian Journal of Family Therapy*, 1982, *4*, 23-26.

Cooklyn, A. Family Therapy in the British context and cultural reflections in practice. *Family Process*, 1978, *17*, 95-105.

Cornwell, M. Beyond the cringe: Family therapy in an Australian context. *Australian Journal of Family Therapy*, 1982, *4*: 55-60.

Fisch, R., Weakland, J., & Segal, L. *The tactics of change: Doing therapy briefly.* San Francisco: Jossey-Bass, 1982.

Haley, J. *Problem solving therapy.* New York: Harper Colophon, 1976.

Haley, J. *Leaving home.* New York: McGraw-Hill, 1980.

Lang, M. Family therapy for the eighties. *Australian Journal of Family Therapy,* 1981, *2,* 48-55.

Liddle, H.A. On the problem of eclecticism: A call for epistemologic clarification and human-scale theories. *Family Process,* 1982, *21,* 243-250.

Liddle, H.A., Breunlin, D.C., Schwartz, R.C., & Constantine, J.A. *An integrative model of structural and strategic family therapy.* Paper presented at the annual conference of the National Council on Family Relations, Milwaukee, Wis., October 1981.

McGoldrick, M., Pearce, J., and Giordano, J. *Ethnicity and family therapy.* New York: Guilford Press. 1982.

Madanes, C. *Strategic family therapy.* San Francisco: Jossey-Bass, 1981.

Madanes, C. & Haley, J. Dimensions of family therapy. *Journal of Nervous and Mental Disease,* 1977, *165,* 88-98.

Minuchin, S. *Families and family therapy.* Cambridge, Mass.: Harvard University Press, 1974.

Minuchin. S., & Fishman, H.C. *Family therapy techniques.* Cambridge, Mass.: Harvard University Press, 1981.

Minuchin, S., Montalvo, B., Guerney, B., Rosman, B., & Shumer, F. *Families of the slums.* New York: Basic Books, 1967.

Montalvo, B. Aspects of live supervision. *Family Process,* 1973, *12,* 343-359.

Papajohn, J. & Spiegel, J. *Transactions in Families.* San Francisco: Jossey-Bass, 1975.

Papp, P. The Greek chorus and other techniques of paradoxical therapy. *Family Process,* 1980, *19,* 45-57.

Skynner, A.C.R. Recent developments in marital therapy. *Journal of Family Therapy,* 1980, *2,* 271-296.

Stagoll, B. Family therapy and Australia: Taking a squiz. *American Journal of Family Therapy,* 1983, *11,* 16-21.

Stanton, M.D. An integrated structural/strategic approach to family therapy. *Journal of Marital and Family Therapy,* 1981, *7,* 427-440.

Topham, M. The song of life: Its words and music. *Australian Journal of Family Therapy,* 1982, *3,* 57-61.

Watzlawick, P., Weakland, J., & Fisch, R. *Change: Principles of problem formation and resolution.* New York: Norton, 1974.

8. Cultural Concepts for Family Therapy

David McGill, PsyD
Smith College
Graduate School of Social Work
Northampton, Massachusetts

This article is derived in part from experience developing and teaching a course entitled "Socio-Cultural Concepts in Clinical Practice" for graduate students at Smith College, from a course on ethnicity and family therapy at the Family Institute of Cambridge, and at a seminar with John Pearce, MD, on ethnicity and family therapy from 1977 to the present.

THE CENTRAL RATIONALE FOR THE CULTURAL EDUCATION OF CLINICIANS
is that life problems, and hence the clinical encounter, occur within a
cultural, ethnic context. Effective psychotherapy engages a life and an
adaptive strategy in process. Clinical competence then logically includes
cultural understanding of the therapeutic encounter and the acquisition of
cultural skills for clinical practice. The major objective of this article is to
facilitate the development of the cultural conceptual skills needed for clinical
practice, using case illustrations and suggesting methods for teaching and
learning these concepts.

DEFINITIONS

The essence of cultural education is teaching and learning about life
strategies. The terms *ethnicity, culture,* and *context* will be used pragmat-
ically (and perhaps idiosyncratically) throughout this article as synonyms
for the central subject: people's life strategies. *Ethnicity* may be understood
as the participation in, and identification with, the life adaptive strategy of a
people. Historically, the term ethnicity has been used broadly for two rather
different subjects. The first concerns minority status, i.e., a primary cultural
ground and its referents. For example: the Roman Empire incorporated
many ethnic peoples. (Romans, of course, were not "ethnic.") A second use
of ethnicity is concerned with cultural *content* (Therstrom, 1980), that is,
patterned life strategies (ethnicities) in which thoughts, feelings, and behaviors occur in cultural context. *Culture* describes the life strategy itself in all
its various components: physical, conceptual, emotional, behavioral, meta-
physical, and so forth. *Context* refers to the ecology of a particular behavior,
which occurs and makes sense within a particular life strategy, life context,
or cultural context.

The word *system* is also linked to ethnicity, culture, context, and life
strategy. The premise of family therapy theory is that individual dysfunction
develops, is understood, and best changed, within a natural system (family);
indeed, systems theorists conceive individual dysfunction as an aspect of
systems dysfunction, and provide treatment for the family system. But what
is the nature of family systems? Are they all different, that is, does the family
therapist treat all families as uniquely *individual* systems, whose internal
parts are analyzed to describe and change system functioning? If so, where
did the families come from, how and why did they get to be the way they
(individually) are? In this article, *system* will be used in ways that suggest a
"systems" rather than an "individual" conception of family systems; that

109

is, family systems themselves derive from and participate in larger cultural systems, or ethnic adaptive life strategies.

REFLECTIONS OF LIFE STRATEGIES IN CLINICAL PRACTICE

A first question might be: What is really meant by life strategy for the clinician and clinical practice? The clinician may be particularly interested in the emotional, cognitive, and behavioral aspects of an adaptive strategy in cultural- or ethno-psychology. Stereotyping is a serious conceptual, methodological, and clinical concern in any discussion of cultural education. Stereotyping might be understood as generalizing out of context and beyond the data. Understanding out of context and beyond the facts is inevitably limited, pejorative and harmful—whatever the intent. For the clinician this implies an obligation to understand a patient within the patients' cultural context, not to generalize beyond what is known, and to retain an attitude of hypothesis and skepticism with regard to one's own understanding of other people. All of the characterizations about life strategies offered here are the hypotheses of the author. The reader is expected *not* to read these as cultural truths, and indeed, to use the author's words and concepts as a model for evolving his or her own words and understanding. For example, the author will offer his characterization of the cultural emotional strategy of British Americans as one of self-contained individualism (McGill & Pearce, 1982). It is hypothesized that British Americans tend to experience themselves as individuals, whole, sufficient, adequate, and contained, within themselves. According to this adaptive strategy, emotional experience is best contained within the individual. Self-contained individualism is the British American idea of how to live, cope, survive, and thrive emotionally. British American families then meet their own cultural requirements for childrearing by raising their children to be and value self-contained individuals. Thus an adaptive life strategy subsumes core values or value orientations that answer basic human questions such as the relationship of individual and group, and preferred relationships to time, the natural world, human nature, and activity (Papajohn & Spiegel, 1975; Spiegel, 1971).

An ethnic life strategy also subsumes the group's core structural expressions (family forms) and the normative functioning throughout the life cycle. That is, implicitly or explicitly, a cultural adaptive strategy communicates the "right" or "good" kind of family: its size, shape, location, patterns of communication and interaction, and so forth. The cultural system contains optimal ways for families to negotiate marriage, childbearing, childrearing, childhood, adolescence, adult love, work, aging, and dying (Carter & McGoldrick, 1980; Falicov & Karrer, 1980; McGoldrick, Pearce & Giordano, 1982).

Life strategies, of course, also imply core "worries," concerns, styles of responding to stress, ways of defining and coping with life's problems. One can infer characteristic defensive styles and preferred "cures" in times of pain, illness, difficulty, and conflict. In short, ethnic group life strategies carry implicit (or explicit) notions about matters of direct concern to the practicing psychotherapist. For example, how might Japanese, Jewish, and British Americans differ in their attribution response to interpersonal conflict? It might be expected that the Japanese American would tend to assign blame (and shame) to himself, having learned that conflict is the misfit, or lack of centeredness, of the individual with society. This response is derived from the general Asian adaptive life strategy of role conformity, centeredness, and balancing of life forces within familial and societal roles. In response to conflict, the Jewish American, however, might first locate the blame externally, that is, on others. This response comes within a general Eastern European Jewish life strategy teaching the sharing of life—life is with and from people. One affirms self and society by making others the cause of discomfort, because that opens the way for others to be the solution to problems; problems are solved by sharing them. The British American response to interpersonal conflict might be the experienced careful, responsible, "objective" weighing and measuring of where the blame might be located—within the self and with other people. The process of determining what share can be attributed to self and what to other is, of course, a self-determined, internal process. In the attribution process to interpersonal conflict, British Americans may have learned to focus on the distinction between self and other; Japanese Americans, on self, and Jewish Americans, on others.

The second educational question might be: How is cultural information actually used in the clinical encounter? The answer, in essence, is that cultural knowledge and skills are brought to the encounter with the patient in the same way that all other clinical education is introduced. The clinicians will use their knowledge of culture and tentative hypotheses about cultural patterns of thinking, feeling, and acting as a basis for recognition of those patterns and their meanings if and when they are presented by the patient. It is never imposed on the patient, nor is one aspect of behavior linked beyond its presentation to a general cultural or ethnic pattern, unless more of the pattern emerges. The use of this knowledge parallels that of developmental psychology, psychopathology, systems functioning, and so forth. All clinical education is used to help the clinician recognize aspects of the patient's experience in some meaningful, potentially beneficial and therapeutic form. Thus the learning and recognizing of patterned life strategies does not suggest the use of ethnic labels in treatment. The clinician will not say, "Aha, that way of thinking (feeling, acting, etc.) is very Japanese (Irish, Armenian, etc.)." On the contrary, the use of particular words by the clinician is, as always, one of careful therapeutic selection with reference to the meaning and use of those words (the clinical intervention) by the patient. Therefore, the clinician does not casually bandy ethnic labels with the patient any more than he would use developmental, analytic, or systems theory diagnostic language. Clinicians may use some of this language and thinking as professional tools to help organize their own thinking and understanding. The language of the therapists' own understanding may be quite different from the language of their caring and careful intervention in clinical practice. This is particularly so with cultural and ethnic labels. The use of an ethnic label by the clinician, in treatment, need never occur, or if so only after the patient has introduced it, and shows that discussing life strategies with respect to their general ethnic patterns will not be experienced as stereotyping, pejorative, or simply foreign to the patient's way of thinking and talking. What the clinician needs to know is the patterns of life strategies themselves, not the ethnic labels that may roughly refer to those patterned life strategies.

A third question might be: Why then should the clinician learn about ethnicity, and why should cultural education discuss ethnicity and the use of ethnic labels? First, ethnicity has created these patterned differences in life strategies. Second, the books, literature, and language of life strategies are categorized by ethnicity. Finally, ethnic identity is a vital component of the life strategies of many American people. Ethnicity and ethnic designations are thus used primarily as a vehicle, a pragmatic form of categorizing and communicating about families to the contemporary American clinical educator and student. Ultimately, the purpose of discussing ethnicity is to provide access to the subject of the life strategies of people and facilitate the effective clinical encounter.

CULTURAL CONTEXT AND THE STAGES OF PSYCHOTHERAPY

In general terms, this article has suggested the what, how, and why of cultural concepts for clinical practice. The next question is: When is cultural knowledge used in the stages of psychotherapy? Related to this are the questions: How is culture important and useful in each of the stages? And what, concretely, is the particular nature of the cross-cultural exchange in each stage in the process of psychotherapy?

The Alliance Phase: Forming the Relationship

Forming a therapeutic relationship has aspects of cultural joining and the formation of a "cultural relationship." The therapist needs to join the patient in the process of his life, and, inevitably, his strategy for living that life. The alliance stage then has to do with validating and affirming, at least via recognition, the family and the cultural context of which they are a part. Part of the *content* of a particular family's life strategy that needs to be understood is, naturally, the family's cultural style of forming trusting relationships, particularly helping relationships. The clinician needs to know what the family expects, within their tradition, that a helper should know and do. For the clinician to accomplish the task of this stage requires, first, this knowledge of what the family expects of a psychotherapist, and second, the capacity to "leave" one's own culture temporarily to follow patient alliance-forming rules. This is a crucial beginning and balancing of the trusting, culturally effective therapeutic alliance. The family members "pay their dues" by trusting the stranger with their pain, dependency, and vulnerability. Therapists pay their dues initially by leaving the comfort of their own cultural assumptions and by demonstrating the capacity to play by the family's cultural rules in getting to know them. The therapist's capacity to be vulnerable and awkward, by trying the family's style and language, is the therapist's message that he understands, values, and validates the family's life strategy. This builds a foundation of trust so that the psychotherapeutic encounter will be culturally syntonic.

For example, the life strategies of Hispanic Americans may contain strong expectations of explicitly demonstrated respect and personalism (*respeto* and *personalismo*) in the formation of trusting relationships. For British Americans respect may be best communicated through an initially impersonal, contractual, technical, negotiation style: respect meaning respecting the need of the self-contained, self-sufficient individual to show himself slowly and carefully. Personal follows impersonal, not the other way around, for British Americans. Jewish American patients may come to therapy with an expectation that emotional expression will be invited, and trust will come from the therapist's demonstration of willingness to engage in intense interpersonal emotional struggle. Black Americans, by virtue of racial minority status and the cultural content of their African American ethnicity, have strategies emphasizing respect for strengths and expect equality of strength in relationships. They tend to expect a therapeutic relationship to be based on recognition of and respect for equal, though perhaps different, strengths. They may distrust a relationship implicitly or explicitly based on shared and sharing vulnerability. Italian Americans tend to be wary of having an outsider (by definition, deeply distrusted) involved in family business. They will measure the therapist against a life strategy of clear boundary maintenance between the family and the outside world. And engaging Irish Americans requires respect for their strategy of moral judging. The therapeutic alliance with Asian Americans may be based on trust through respect (avoiding the danger of inducing shame) by means of an indirect, subtle, carefully paced meeting style. This will convey to Asian families that psychotherapy will be syntonic with the cultural strategy of role maintenance and will not require direct expressions of vulnerability which risk loss of face. These contrasting life strategies and styles of meeting suggest an enormous range of possible cultural hits and misses during the joining process.

Culture in the Problem Definition Stage in Psychotherapy

One aspect of the process of understanding or diagnosing the presenting problem in psychotherapy is cultural. Going to a psychotherapist for help when in distress suggests that the family and their life strategy are stressed, upset, not working adequately, or not adapting to current needs. The family then enters therapy not only "culturally vulnerable," as seen in the alliance phase where the vulnerability comes from encounter with the culturally different therapist. The presentation in therapy can also be understood as cultural/emotional distress. That is, the cultural strategy itself and its viability (at least in part) is brought into question with the pain of the presenting problem, symptom, or dysfunction. The patient's stress response style and experience of presenting problem and symptom are themselves likely to be derived from the patient's life strategy. Life strategies (ethnicities) pattern location, experience, and expression of pain (Zborowski, 1969). Whatever the cultural form of pain, the presentation of individual or family life difficulties brought to psychotherapy are often manifestations of cultural coping styles that are carried too rigidly or to an extreme. Here the theme of time is introduced. Adaptive life strategies are, of course, dynamic and ever-changing, in parallel with internal (human system) and environmental changes, and with evolving ecological transactions (Spiegel, 1971).

Symptoms often represent the expression of psychological distress and act as a form of ineffective cultural perseveration—a response to stress repeated outside or beyond its time and circumstances of effectiveness. For example, British American emotional self-containment may be exaggerated as a coping response to stress, for example, a death in the family. Guest (1977) illustrates this exaggerated British American self-containment and emotional withdrawal in response to tragic loss.

The life strategy must be understood to gain access to the meaning, process, and development of the presenting problem. The problem develops within its cultural context. The cultural aspect of diagnosis suggests making sense of the presenting problem and describing it in language that is culturally syntonic and useful to the family.

Of course, the best way to find out what the family members think is wrong is to ask: "What is your idea (theory, understanding, etc.) of what is wrong? How did it come about? What have you tried to do about it? What do you think needs to be done now?" There is, of course, a well-documented range of problems presented to the psychotherapist; however, there are also predictable life pattern/ethnic core ideas about "what's wrong" in difficult times, which may be presented across the spectrum of "objective" problem categories. There are ethnic patterns to what families will say. For example, Eastern European Jewish families are likely to believe that they lack adequate understanding of the depth and complexity of emotional experience due to a blocking of interpersonal sharing and expression—a failure to adequately share life with people. Hispanic Americans will often experience a basic loss of respect or warm familism, perhaps due to cultural/generational change and extrafamilial exposure through recent (one or two generation) immigration. Italian American families typically experience failure to "keep it in the family" as a failure of family loyalty. These "understandings" are the generic, cultural explanation—the problem behind the problem that often will surface for patients in these groups.

The Intervention—Culture in the Treatment

Once a culturally meaningful understanding of the patient's problem has been mutually developed, the process of implementing a culturally syntonic intervention or "cure" can be addressed. The line between understanding and response is typically a fine one. Traditionally the patient will not only have core ideas of what is wrong when things go wrong, but will also have patterns of stress responses, or preferred "cures" for troubles that are central aspects of their cultural life adaptive strategies. It is at this stage of therapy, when the therapist has successfully moved toward the patient culturally—the therapist has demonstrated the capacity to be culturally flexible and to relate in a variety of ways—that the patient is given the opportunity to respond to his problematic experience in new ways. Change in psychotherapy might in part be considered a change or modification in the cultural life strategy of the patient. This will involve learning to restore, expand, or modify the cultural stress response repertoire.

What then is the style and process of helping clients try something new, or helping them restore a forgotten response or retrieve an old resource to cope with the current issue? Often the process of helping the client change begins by framing the change within traditional culturally syntonic language. The client is urged to "keep doing what you are doing" which will form a foundation for adding something new or trying something different. In each case the new is presented as (and must at some level truly be) an extension of the "old" cultural stress response. Many theories of learning and change (cognitive psychology, adult education learning theory, etc.) stress the importance of affirming the base of what the learner or client already has, as the necessary precondition for assimilating and then accommodating a new response. For example, British Americans will be supported by the therapist in their struggle to be adequately individual and self-contained in their response to stressful circumstances. Once British American clients are convinced that the therapist really "understands" what they are trying to do to solve the problem (i.e, to be restored to adequate self-sufficiency), then they may be able to "hear" the therapist's suggestion that the path to restored individualism may be through practice of more interpersonal emotional sharing, more contact, and less isolation (emotional isolation being the hazard of the British American life strategy carried to an extreme). The therapist will then introduce and monitor the change of the British American in careful, step-by-step, individually oriented instructions and discussion. In other words, psychotherapeutic change is partly cultural change. Change is grounded on a validation of the family's current life strategy, conceived as a modification or extension of that strategy, and introduced in a style that is culturally syntonic with the current life strategy. The change itself is likely to be a balancing of the individual or family's traditional response, or a "cure" for the hazardous consequences of the cultural strategy when it is held to an extreme. The core therapeutic intervention for British-Americans—whatever the presenting problem—may be to reduce emotional isolation and modify a strategy of exaggerated emotional self-sufficiency.

A core cultural change strategy with Jewish families may be to expand the syntonic process of interpersonal sharing and emotional analysis to include attention to the many aspects of their own and others' *behavior* (as well as feelings) with an opening to modify their interpersonal behavior (as well as their feelings about others). Work with Black Americans may extend a focus on their strategies of empowerment to include and master areas of vulnerability and powerlessness for themselves and others. Hispanic and Asian Americans may be assisted by the therapist acting as a "culture broker" (Spiegel, 1971), or "culture intermediary" (Falicov, 1982), to negotiate relationships between the family and mainstream America. This is done through a culturally syntonic reinterpretation of cross-generational differences and conflicts, as all being efforts toward family cultural loyalty and maintenance in the face of the pressures of migration on family functioning (Sluzki, 1979).

Change in family therapy with Italians may involve their learning to more flexibly accommodate the inside/outside family boundary by using outsiders (beginning with the therapist) to maintain rather than threaten that value.

For example, the therapist (although a cultural outsider) may help repair relations between a young adult single professional Italian daughter and her family. However, a therapist who is *not* culturally syntonic may alienate the same client. A British American therapist was somewhat confused and exasperated by the young Italian professional woman's endless complaints about her mother. The therapist heard what he assessed as extreme "enmeshed, intrusive" behavior, though he may have been wise enough not to verbalize this "diagnosis" to his client. However, after another seemingly endless session in the same vein, the therapist dropped his professional reluctance to "advise" and said to his east coast patient, "Why don't you just move to Denver?" This is a classic example of cultural countertransference, which in this case ended the therapeutic relationship. The British American therapist, of course, was only suggesting the obvious British American cure—move on and become a self-contained, self-sufficient individual. He had no idea that his suggestion prescribed the equivalent of cultural "death" for his Italian patient. She, naturally, realized the therapist had no understanding of her, her problem, or her family and that it was "dangerous" to continue seeing him.

Irish families may feel culturally joined when their moral surveillance strategy is validated, as a basis for suggesting that they move on personally and interpersonally rather than be blocked or paralyzed by the inevitable occasional experience of moral failure that comes with their style.

All of the above examples of core ethnic "cures" are offered only as the author's suggestive hypotheses. Students and therapists will want to review the literature and their own experience to develop a personal formulation of core ethnic adaptive strategies. These examples are offered only to illustrate how cultural forces are active in the change phase of psychotherapy.

To develop cultural competence, the therapists need (1) to know the range of specific ethnic cultural adaptation strategies for themselves and their clients, (2) to be able to use a variety of strategies, both to join the patient and to model learning new strategies, and (3) to become more "multicultural" in response to life problems. This multicultural use of self is the primary cultural competence of the professional psychotherapist.

Culture in the Ending Phase of Psychotherapy

The ending of psychotherapy also has an important cultural aspect. The task here is to reconnect and restore the patient or family to their larger world. In parallel with the alliance phase, the patient's original life strategy is again validated, this time incorporating the changes and modifications introduced in psychotherapy. For change to endure and work, it must in some sense be truly accommodated and not experienced as a discontinuous break with former experience, functioning, and circumstances, however difficult they may have been. For new adaptive strategies to work, they must work after and apart from the interaction with the therapist; that is, they must be truly owned, culturally, by the patient.

For example, after psychotherapy, the British American needs to continue to feel adequately self-contained, at the same time he has integrated much more interpersonal emotional expressiveness. In other words, British Americans learn not only that sharing is compatible with their need for self-containment (contrary to pre-therapeutic understanding) but that sharing may support their core need to experience individual adequacy.

Ending may not always be comfortable for the therapist, since it comes, most likely, in the cultural style of the patient. Irish families, for example, may end abruptly, without clear acknowledgment of having been helped, not wishing to "spoil" the therapist with praise, and affirming continued discomfort and embarrassment with therapy itself—even with successful therapy. Jewish patients may leave complaining of the inadequate "depth" of emotional analysis while sustaining their improved behavior. British Americans may end abruptly when business is done rather than "process" their separation with the therapist. Italian Americans may "fire" their successful therapist to ritually reaffirm their basic cultural faith in the mistrust of outsiders. Hispanics and Asians may show some reexpression of core values in termination by demonstrating their restored experience of respect and role centeredness. Poles may end by returning to such hard work that they have "no more time" for therapy.

The ending phase of therapy affirms new paths to old goals. Psychotherapy, in this view, does not change culture, or treat the cultural strategy itself as invalid. On the contrary, psychotherapy is, in a sense, deeply culturally conservative, with cultural affirmation and expansion as the only effective, as well as ethical, path to improved adaptation.

THE CROSS-CULTURAL PROCESS IN THE STAGES OF PSYCHOTHERAPY

It is now possible to summarize the "cross-cultural" process at each of the stages of psychotherapy. First, in order to form the therapeutic alliance, the therapist leaves his cultural world and life strategy and moves to join, and thereby affirm, the life strategy of the family. Second, the therapist and family jointly decipher the current presenting problem in the language and context of the family. The therapist brings to this effort many kinds of understandings, including those of his own family of origin, those of psychological theory and training, and those of experience with other patients with similar presentations. This multicultural perspective is joined with each family's ideas and language to describe the problem. Third, the therapist helps the family move outward and try on other problem responses, giving the family an active multicultural capacity to respond to their problems. In this change phase, the therapist's own (different) life strategy may be a most valuable tool. The family tries on new strategies, modifying and enhancing, never replacing, their own. Finally, in ending, the family is helped to reaffirm their increased strategic capacity within their own world. This will be maintained separate from and after contact with the "foreign world" of psychotherapy.

FOREST OR TREES: CULTURAL INTENSITY IN PSYCHOTHERAPY

In addition to the issues discussed above concerning the what, how, why, and when of cultural concepts in psychotherapy, there is a final question: In which cases are cultural concepts important, and to what degree may cultural understanding relate to the type of problem and mix of therapist/patient background?

Cultural forces are most obviously important in the kind of "special" cases where there are conspicuous cultural differences. This is immediately apparent in work with immigrants where the therapist does not speak the patient's language. In these cases, all parties can recognize the need for, at least, some cultural explaining. Differences in life strategies may become primary content in work with obviously cross-cultural couples and families, such as mixed racial families by marriage, or adoption (see Faulkner and Kich's article in this volume). The focus is on *within* family system differences, as well as on family therapist differences. Although cultural issues may be more subtle with other families, this article has attempted to develop a framework for including cultural perspectives designed for all psychotherapy—for "everyday" as well as with "special" case psychotherapy; for psychotherapy where cultural differences within the family system or between family and therapist are not an obvious issue. Furthermore, the therapist can bring all the requisite cultural knowledge and skills to work on a case without ever labeling the work as cultural, or the change as a new cultural style of coping.

REFERENCES

Bowen, M. *Family therapy in clinical practice.* New York: Jason Aronson, 1978.

Carter, E. & McGoldrick, M. *The family life cycle: A framework for family therapy.* New York: Gardner Press, 1980.

Falicov, C. Mexican-American families. In M. McGoldrick, J. Pearce, & G. Giordano (Eds.), *Ethnicity and family therapy.* New York: Guilford Press, 1982.

Falicov, C., & Karrer, B. Cultural variations in the family life cycle. In E. Carter & M. McGoldrick (Eds.), *The family life cycle: A framework for family therapy.* New York: Gardner Press, 1980.

Greeley, A. *Ethnic drinking subcultures.* New York: Praeger, 1980.

Guest, J. *Ordinary people.* New York: Ballantine, 1977.

Jones, E. *The life and work of Sigmund Freud.* New York: Basic Books, 1961.

McGill, D., & Pearce, J. British American families. In M. McGoldrick, J. Pearce, & G. Giordano (Eds.), *Ethnicity and family therapy.* New York, Guilford Press, 1982.

McGoldrick, M., Pearce, J., & Giordano, J. *Ethnicity and family therapy.* New York, Guilford Press, 1982.

Minuchin, S. *Families and family therapy.* Cambridge, Mass.: Harvard University Press, 1974.

Papajohn, J., & Spiegel, J. *Transactions in families: A modern approach for resolving cultural and generational conflicts.* San Francisco: Jossey-Bass, 1975.

Sluzki, C. Migration and family conflict. *Family Process,* 1979, *18*(4), 379-390.

Spiegel, J. *Transactions: The interplay between individual, family and society.* New York: Science House, 1971.

Therstrom, S., Orlov, A., & Handlin, O. *Harvard encyclopedia of American ethnic groups.* Cambridge, Mass.: Harvard University Press, 1980.

Zborowski, M., & Herzog, E. *Life is with people.* New York: Schocken Books, 1952.

Zborowski, M. *People in pain.* San Francisco: Jossey-Bass, 1969.

9. On Becoming a Culturally Conscious Family Therapist

Jay Lappin, ACSW
Philadelphia Child Guidance Clinic
Philadelphia, Pennsylvania

The author wishes to thank Braulio Montalvo, Jorge Colapinto, and Sam Scott for their cross-cultural insights and wisdom, and Marcia Vitiello for editorial assistance. Special thanks to Molly Layton for her clarity and patience in helping me rewrite the innumerable drafts. And most of all, thanks to my wife Joyce.

WORKING WITH FAMILIES FROM ANOTHER CULTURE IS A CHALLENGE to the clinician. Ignorance of the culture's norms, values, and expectations can organize the clinician toward inactivity—being too courteous—or toward disrespect—by not being courteous enough. If there was ever a potential no-win situation for the therapist, this is it. Yet when one begins to think at another level—the level of process—similarities among families begin to emerge.

To enter a family system, unless it is one's own, is to enter a different culture. To be successful, the clinician must begin to act as a systemic anthropologist, observing the rules and rituals that govern the family's behavior. The therapeutic goal becomes a search for the elements of strength within that particular family culture that offer the potential for change. As the family makes use of previously untapped resources, the therapist's involvement becomes less and less until, like any good anthropologist, he leaves the culture behind and intact. The family retains its cultural integrity. The therapist moves on to yet another culture, another family, and must be content with the privilege of being an expendable part of another's life.

The problem, however, is that few clinicians are trained as anthropologists. Clinicians tend to view anthropology as either too broad or too passive to be useful. Those of us in the trenches with huge caseloads, productivity quotas, and budget cuts, are not inclined to muse over the cultural implications of the latest *National Geographic*. We want something that works, something that makes our jobs just a touch easier. A cultural framework can sometimes do just that. It is an opportunity to see beyond a family's struggle and offer a perspective that is respectful and challenging. It is a way of thinking that calls for a certain posture and attitude on the part of the clinician. It is not simply another tactic or weapon in the clinician's arsenal. Rather it is an attitude in which aesthetics and utility meet.

Family therapy and systems theory are coming of age. There are paradigms that teach us to look beyond the family's presenting problem to examine the world of rules and patterns of behavior. These theories have taught us to be contextual, and even ecological, in explaining behavior. Yet despite this contextual mandate, systems therapists remain culturally myopic. This is not totally the fault of therapists. Few training programs or graduate schools attend to the cultural aspects of family work. McGoldrick, Pearce, and Giordano (1982) rightly point out that "most of us have gone through our entire professional educations with hardly a word mentioned about ethnicity" (p. xv). The question, then, is how can one go about becoming more culturally sensitized?

This article will address the pitfalls and positives of such a cross-cultural journey. Specific recommendations, highlighted by case examples, will demonstrate that the road is not as rocky as one might think. Both systemic and personal aspects of cross-cultural work will be raised and discussed. But first, a story.

ON BEING MORE HUMAN

In *Myth, Symbol, and Culture,* Clifford Geertz (1971) recalls how he and his wife, both anthropologists, came to know the people of Bali. Arriving "wistful and eager to please," the Geertzes found themselves in the midst of an indifferent reception, feeling vaguely disembodied as if they "simply did not exist." The Geertzes, however, did know something about the Balinese, namely their love for cockfighting. Cockfighting is so much a part of Balinese life that it is included in metaphors about eating, fighting, relationships, land, and love. In any event, the Geertzes had been in Bali for about 10 days. Still very much "invisible," they were watching, along with hundreds of villagers, a huge cockfight in the village square. Although cockfights were illegal, everyone seemed to feel that, for whatever reason, this one would not be raided. In Geertz's words, "they were wrong." The "pulisi" roared up, waving guns, scattering the assembled masses. Into the dust and mayhem ran the two American anthropologists. Following a stranger, they ducked down an alley and ran into a small courtyard where, without a word, the man's wife began to serve tea. A policeman, searching for the village chief, arrived shortly. To his amazement, he found the two Americans quietly sipping tea with the villager. Questioning their activities, he was met with a righteous verbal assault by the Balinese accomplice, who proceeded to explain that they had been discussing life in Bali for a book to be published in America. Confused, the policeman left; and so did the Geertzes. Much to their surprise, the next day the couple found that they were no longer "invisible." Instead they were the focus of a great deal of warmth, interest, and amusement. The villagers incessantly and gently teased the Geertzes and were tickled that the couple had not shown their "Distinguished Visitor Papers." The author points out that "in Bali, to be teased is to be accepted. It was the turning point so far as our relationship was concerned, and we were quite literally 'in'." This is joining at its finest.

RISK AND RESPECT

Hillary Greene, a young white female therapist, was seeing a Muslim single-parent family for the first time. Mother was dressed in traditional garb: long black robes covering her body; a black veil and hood over her face and head; only her sad eyes a clue to her identity and pain. The therapist, anxious because this was her first Muslim family, started the session by asking mother about her dress. It was a risk, yet one mother seemed to appreciate. She patiently explained that she was a follower of Muhammad. She said that she covered her body to minimize the "sexual stuff" people thought about when they saw someone dressed "like you." The therapist, dressed casually, smiled and nodded. Mother then explained that her son, also in Muslim garb, was called Daud, which means "man of distinction."

In this instance, the therapist, with mother's help, had successfully walked the tightrope between risk and respect. The balance has to do with the attitude the therapist conveys—one of asking for the family's help while, at the same time, offering help. Cultural questioning is the start of a process that can begin to challenge old rules, roles, and narrow definitions of self. These have a history of being held intact by cultural restraints: "Our people don't ever . . ., We always . . ." and so forth. The questioning acknowledges the fact that the family knows more about themselves than does the therapist. But at the same time it can also challenge nonadaptive coping mechanisms. Braulio Montalvo (a colleague at the Philadelphia Child Guidance Clinic and fellow cross-cultural traveler) feels that a therapist can use a family as a guide into their world.

The guiding process can become muddled, however, if the therapist and family are culturally syntonic. Both family and therapist expect the therapist to know the territory. Indeed, there is a welcome mat that is extended to someone who is "one of us." The advantages of being from the same culture as the family are many: familiarity with customs; knowledge of roles, rules, and expectations; and acquaintance with language, rituals, values, and etiquette. There are times, however, when the welcome mat may wear thin. This is true especially if the therapist, who is of the same culture, ignores or steps inappropriately into sacred ground. In these instances, the therapist will be faced with the cultural equivalent of "you should know better."

Cross-cultural therapists, on the other hand, are often given "diplomatic immunity" by the family. A little ignorance can go a long way. Therapists who ask, "Can you please help me?", with a foreign accent, activate the family's natural helping response. They highlight differences, and thus put the family in the position of being one-up.

Joining the therapeutic system at the level of mutual accommodation and recognition of differences establishes common points of contact. The Muslim family, for example, allowed the therapist a brief trip into their world. The therapist's sense of risk was balanced by her position of respect. Maintaining this position allows the family to reveal which aspects of its system are crucial. It becomes the safety net that prevents fatal falls.

Yet despite these assurances, there are those who would suggest that cultural questioning will hamper their position as "expert." These are the people who act as if a Muslim's robes are the same as a pantsuit from J.C. Penney. Pursuing obvious cultural differences, whether it be clothing, accent, or appearance, does not compromise the therapist as the leader of the therapeutic system. Rather, the role is enhanced and legitimized. We are not such a melting pot that we know everything about each other simply because we're all in the same stew. Families know this. Therapists lose credibility when they act as if the obvious does not exist. The important point to remember, as in any systems work, is to read the feedback. This means recognizing that some families may be anxiously trying to shed their cultural baggage in an attempt to identify with their new surroundings. In this case, the therapist would still need to pursue differences, but with an ear toward tempering responses in a way that respects the family's level of comfort. In the case of the Muslim woman, the therapist reduced differences and increased human-to-human contact. She did this because she continued to get green lights from the family system. In this way, as she questioned mother, trust was established; and a fearful client returned for her second session.

Reading feedback in cross-cultural work can also be a very humbling experience, as therapists who engage in this work will quickly discover. While teaching a group of older Vietnamese, Cambodian, and Thai refugee men, I plodded vainly along trying to get the group to answer my Socratic-style questions (a technique that had worked with a younger, mixed Indochinese group). They looked at me silently, with baleful eyes, as I struggled through the hour. Finally, one man raised his hand. "Yes!" I exclaimed. Quietly he started, "Mr. Jay, we don't have class like this in Vietnam. In our country teacher speak. We listen; take notes. You give test." I was mortified. I looked to the group and asked, "Is that right?" A silent yes. A little embarrassed, I thanked the man and said I was going out of the room, that when I came back things would be different. I returned and began to write on the board, "Test next week." I then began lecturing. No questions. They loved it, and I learned.

STEREOTYPES

Blind faith and respect, however, are not enough to navigate the complicated sea of cross-cultural waters. In order to be effective, one needs to know the nuances of group and intra-group differences. This is not to say that cultural qualities and patterns can be reduced into neat categories. What it does mean, however, is forming a knowledge base about the culture with which you are working. It means becoming attuned to the macro- and micro-aspects of therapy and the culture. Characteristics such as body posture, voice tone, and facial expressions carry greater valence in cross-cultural work. When people have difficulty in understanding *what* you say, you need to be very careful of *how* you say it. Issues of class, caste, income status, and especially roles, are critical variables in cross-cultural work. This is particularly true with families who have recently immigrated. Fine-tuning cultural sensitivity strengthens the clinician's position by demonstrating to the family that he does not simply lump all members of one ethnic group into the same pot. A person who is from Brooklyn, New York will appreciate not being treated as if he is from Grovetown, Georgia, much the same as someone from Grovetown, Georgia will appreciate not being treated as if he is from Brooklyn, New York.

Being familiar with cultural facts and idiosyncrasies, however, does not guarantee immunity from the negative aspects of stereotypes. Wanting to avoid stereotyping is a legitimate concern, because stereotypes have been badly abused (McGoldrick, Pearce, & Giordano, 1982). Fear of potential abuse should temper, but not dissuade, clinicians from venturing into cross-cultural waters. Stereotypes need to be thought of as a starting point, a broad paradigm. They provide the framework to begin an ongoing success. As the therapist learns more about the culture, new information is introduced, and old ideas are challenged. Stereotyping needs to move toward greater complexity, not simplicity. Simplistic stereotyping is the area in which abuse occurs.

HOUSE ETHNICS

Warning: Fear of stereotyping can lead to the creation of "house ethnics." Agencies with good intentions may unwittingly avoid cross-cultural

work because they feel that it is not respectful for ethnic groups to see
therapists of another culture. Families are automatically assigned to therapists of similar ethnic heritage, and neither client nor therapist is asked if this
is preferred. Montalvo (1974) has written about the good intentions of
agencies going awry. He also cautions us about the house ethnic phenomenon: "In the barrios, community people wanted a professional, a
doctor, regardless of race, who felt they could *do* something for them . . .
There are many who felt that seeing a para-professional of their own race
was somehow cheating them. The important thing was to get professional
help, otherwise they could simply go to a neighbor or a relative" (personal
communication, December 1974). These concerns return us to the old social
work axiom of starting where the client "is at." To assume that each ethnic
group wants to be seen by their own representative denies them the right of
having a say in who treats them. A preferable situation is to ask the family
what they prefer. Also, ethnic therapists should be given the opportunity to
work outside of their own cultural sphere.

   This may mean that therapists have to become a bit like anthropologists,
observing and experiencing another culture before jumping into cross-
cultural work. Structural family therapy and other systems approaches offer
a framework for beginning this process.

STRUCTURAL FAMILY THERAPY

   Another concept we can borrow from anthropologists is accommodating
to the pace of the family. This may mean a protracted joining phase, a home
visit, or other means of acculturating the therapeutic system. Minuchin and
Fishman (1981) state that "joining is the glue that holds the therapeutic
system together" (p. 32). A "given" in cross-cultural work is that the glue
takes longer to dry.

   While structural family therapy is usually seen as a brief therapy model, I
have found that it can also be an effective tool when used at the slower pace
that cross-cultural work demands, particularly with Indochinese families. I
would agree with Shon and Ja (1982), who found "the structural family
therapy model quite helpful because of its emphasis on actively restructuring
the interactions in the family to create change rather than relying on direct
and open expressions of feelings as a necessary part of the process of
therapy" (p. 227).

   Structural family therapy is rooted with an emphasis on process, complementarity, and how the family changes shape in adapting to life events. It

gives useful, concrete pegs for making clinical assessment and setting treatment goals. A here-and-now process-oriented framework has particular value with families who have limited English skills. One day, as an experiment in a class of Indochinese case workers, we taped a group of Lao who made a role play of a family. They told us none of the case details, did not identify family members (including the identified patient), and did not state the presenting problem. Just to keep us honest, they did the role play in Laotian. After the role play, we played a kind of "structural family feud" and attempted to have the non-Lao class members compete to identify who was who. Surprisingly, had the class really been on TV, they would have won the Bahamas vacation and twin Toyotas. Their accuracy was uncanny. The reasons, I believe, were (1) they knew the roles within the culture, and (2) they focused on process.

Creating structural changes should not be totally compromised by the idiosyncrasies of culture. The issue is how to use the culture as a means to a structural end. Goal assessment then needs to filter through a cultural lens, but process is still process in any language. Take the case, for example, in which a family presents with dysfunctional overinvolvement. The therapist's goal would be to increase the distance between overinvolved members and strengthen boundaries in the system. How that is done and how much that is done depend on the values of the culture. In other words, if the cultural norm places a positive value on being physically and emotionally close, one will need to gear efforts at increasing distance accordingly. What is "distance" in one culture may have a very different meaning in another. An Irish family, for example, might be very comfortable with minimal extended kin contact. An Italian family might experience this same amount of contact as being cut off from the kin network. Too much cultural dissonance results in families dropping out of treatment. Too little dissonance will result in the family adopting the therapist.

Once again, success has to do with balancing the risks of pushing old patterns to change, increasing complexity, and, on the other side of the scale, communicating respect—allowing people to save face. Cultural information can also provide the lumber to reframe a presenting problem. The Muslim boy mentioned earlier had been labeled as "stupid" by his stepfather, who felt the boy was excessively quiet. The label was challenged by the therapist when she told mother that "men of distinction are thoughtful and don't give quick answers." Mother was then able to be more patient with her son, and the pattern of her rushing in to fill his silences was broken. The therapist's cultural tracking uncovered the language of the family and made it available for reframing the problem. An attitude of cultural sensitivity can be helpful with a wide range of problems and families.

A THERAPEUTIC INSTANCE

The session was with a 25-year-old Puerto Rican heroin addict. He was detoxing. During the session he repeatedly complained of pain that made him sweat with discomfort. At one point I found myself asking the addict's permission to touch his clammy stomach and invited the family to do the same. It was not until after I left the session and talked with Braulio Montalvo that I realized I had been part of a culturally sanctioned transaction. I had experienced a cross-cultural altered state. I had entered a world where high priority is given to expressing and experiencing physical pain. Empathy had been the correct move, syntonic with the family's cultural values. Father, who used not talking to the son as a way of showing his disapproval of the son's drug habit, took part in the ritual. Through the common bond of appreciating physical discomfort, father and son were joined. For a brief moment, therapeutic goals, process, and culture were in harmony. The addict was removed from his scapegoat position, the family was literally touching his pain, and cultural values both permitted and enhanced the intervention. Concrete metaphors carry increased weight in the therapeutic system when structural goals can be framed in the family's own language, particularly the language of their values.

Fortunately, the experience with the Puerto Rican addict and his family took place at the beginning of the research project. I was able to make full use of its valuable lessons about (1) working at the family's pace, (2) the importance of home visits, and (3) doing more subsystem work. With the addict population, it also provided an opportunity to establish a modicum of trust in families where trust is in deficit. This is not to say that the structural model is the "end all" for doing cross-cultural work. McGoldrick et al. (1982) provide suggestions for specific models with specific cultural groups.

The important thing to remember is that any theory is only a framework, a starting point. One must always be open to being surprised. A Vietnamese woman was describing her difficulty in counseling American women about birth control. Because of my years of experience with the Vietnamese, I assumed that she was embarrassed about such an intimate topic and, confidently, asked if this was so. She said no, it was not embarrassment at all. The problem was a different one. From where she sat, Americans display a less pronounced class structure. In Vietnam, she said, she would know just how to act and what to say based on the person's class. Here, she has no such grounding. This Vietnamese student had been in the United States for over 5 years, yet she still was feeling the gentle tug of her homeland. This brings us to another important issue if one is considering cross-cultural work: namely, knowing at what stage the family is in the acculturation process.

ACCULTURATION

Acculturation information is particularly important when working with families who have recently immigrated. Carlos Sluzki (1979) provides an excellent framework in his article on migration and family conflict. He describes a five-stage model for assessing where a family is in the migration process and discusses specific points and issues that reflect the family's coping mechanism that "unchains different types of conflicts and symptoms." According to Sluzki, the five stages are (1) preparatory stage, (2) migration, (3) period of overcompensation, (4) period of crisis decompensation, and (5) trans-generational phenomena. Each state requires assessment and interventions geared for the specific phase the family is experiencing. Sluzki goes on to say that the process of migration presents "outstanding regularities" that, when taken to the level of process, cut across cultural distinctions, leaving a "culture-free model." This model not only cuts across cultural lines, but also helps in working with American families that are experiencing the migration phenomena because of corporate moves or other changes in life circumstances.

What Sluzki is suggesting is a kind of stress inventory, a migratory Holmes and Rahe test. It offers a way to assess family stress, predict future stresses, and guide clinical treatment. Many systems therapists tend to avoid questions that have a historical ring to them, fearing they may become trapped by the family's history. Minuchin, for instance, is notorious for his avoidance of history and his focus on present functioning. In cross-cultural work, however, a little history can go a long way. Tracking the family's migratory history not only joins the therapist to the family, through accompanying them on their journey, but also points to their migratory developmental stage and illustrates how the family functions under stress.

Sluzki points out that most families are not even aware of the stress of migrating. An appealing aspect to his model is that it is nonpejorative, so focus on migratory stress can provide a new frame for symptomatic behavior. Instead of the members feeling attacked or blamed for symptoms, a common fear of people in family therapy, the context is attacked. The adaptiveness of the family is challenged, rather than the members themselves.

This position is similar to Minuchin's stance of attacking the homeostatic rules that prevent a family from achieving greater complexity and more individual autonomy. This position produces two effects: it joins, through challenge to dysfunctional rules, while simultaneously unbalancing, as the therapist sides with the family. The therapist's weight is put on the functional side of the family in their attempt to accommodate to an immovable object, that is, their new context. The family structure must change shape with rules and roles modified to fit their new context. The fact that they have succeeded in arriving at their new home bolsters the therapist's conviction that they can succeed.

The flip side of cross-cultural work is the danger of using cultural pegs too rigidly. Sluzki used the example of a therapist who conducted himself in an excessively formal manner when working with a Japanese family. The family then thought that this is what the therapist expected, and responded in kind. This further confirmed the therapist's notion that the Japanese are a very formal people. If the therapist is too distant, by virtue of an overly respectful position, families feel as if the therapist is responding only to the stereotype of their ethnic group and not to them as people. This is unfortunate and can result in families dropping out of treatment, which only further supports the therapist's contention that work with other ethnic groups is not rewarding or worth the time. It also serves to maintain the problem of house ethnics.

Regardless of the choice of model, therapists working cross-culturally need to raise their awareness and follow Sluzki's suggestions. In structural family therapy, for example, where emphasis is typically more here-and-now, some judicious systemic history taking can be extremely helpful. This can be done, very simply, by tracking the family's migratory process. Among the questions that can help the therapist assess the family's stage of acculturation are: How long have you been in the United States? How did you decide to move here? Who made these decisions? How did you tell the children? Were they involved in deciding? Who was the move hardest on? At the same time, the reality of the new context's impingement on the family's context is brought home to the family. Furthermore, the observant therapist will see both strengths and structure and can begin to formulate goals and new frames for symptomatic behavior. Once again, these questions can apply to American families on the move, as well as families immigrating from other cultures.

If the clinician does have the opportunity to work cross-culturally, issues around language and translation may arise.

ON INTERPRETERS AND TRANSLATORS

Gauri Deshpande (1979) summarizes the dilemma of the translator: "There is a standard pun based upon the similarity of the two Latin words for traitor and translator. Since I happily belong to the latter category, I cannot say I am flattered by thus being associated with the former" (p. 2). In cross-cultural work, the temptation to use a translator is often great, but Deshpande's words should alert our systemic sensitivities.

On the positive side, a translator offers expediency, language, and culture and, some would argue, comfort for family and therapist. If at all possible, however, the cross-cultural therapist will want to work without a translator. This does not mean that translators are not worth their weight in gold in families without any English skills. Clearly, in such families, a translator is a necessity. Yet one should not choose a translator simply because he knows the language. Deshpande talks about how the terms translator and interpreter are "continuously used to mean either, that they come together with such an air of inevitability . . . that it has come time for the real translators, the chewers of nails over the exact nuance, the shedders of tears over shapes of meaning . . . to work hard, diligently, and ruthlessly to expose and root out the interpreters from among them." He goes on to say that "if as the sages tell us, the way to Nirvana lies in the subjugation of the ego, then surely translators are already halfway there . . ." (p. 2). Yet Deshpande's agony over interpreting versus translating should alert us to certain dangers. The mere fact of the addition of another person in the room makes for increased complexity. It is built-in triangulation on several levels. Here are six reasons to avoid using translators (these reasons apply especially to interpreters):

1. It puts the family in the one-down position at a time when they need to be one-up (Lappin & Scott, 1982).
2. Communication is through, not to, someone. This diminishes the intensity of any possible cross-cultural dyads.
3. The translator becomes central to the therapy by virtue of his switchboard position.
4. The therapist can never be sure if the family is responding to what the therapist said or what the translator thought the therapist said or how the translator thought the therapist said it.

5. Sometimes translators "interpret" the meaning of the therapist's words into what the interpreter thought the therapist meant to say or what the family wants to hear.
6. The translator is not only at the apex of a systemic triangle, but a cultural one as well.

The use of a translator dilutes the richness of cross-cultural experience for everyone, family and therapist alike. Pragmatics, of course, do not always afford us the luxury of working without a translator. Budget cuts, though, may reduce money for translator services. However, this might not be so bad; more of us may get to travel abroad without leaving the office. But be forewarned: it is a slow boat.

A cross-cultural perspective can only be appreciated if it is experienced. The first way for a therapist to experience a cross-cultural perspective is to see families of other cultures, and to simply become aware of the cultural aspects of the groups with whom he is working. The second method (and the two are by no means mutually exclusive) is to become aware of one's own cultural heritage.

TASTING THE SOUP

Americans are notoriously ethnocentric. Some might choose to combat this ethnocentricity with books. While this is certainly both interesting and useful, it should not be the sole method of cross-cultural travel. To paraphrase Salvador Minuchin, one must "taste the soup" to know it. Very literally, a culturally aware therapist must do just that. Go out into the community; meet people; go to the stores; eat what the people eat; make home visits. Margaret Mead had a wonderful and effective way of assimilating other cultures by becoming "proficient" in the culture for one day. She would learn enough of the language to catch a bus, buy her meals, go to the bathroom, and so forth. Agencies might begin to think about sponsoring events such as community dinners that would allow people to join other cultures through the universal ritual of eating. Agencies could also pay a family that has become acculturated, but is still in touch with its roots, to come to the clinic to be interviewed.

During the early days of a foster care demonstration project, a group of "famous foster mothers" were identified by state child care workers. The women were invited to the clinic and paid to be interviewed and videotaped. The purpose was to see if the mothers displayed consistent qualities that would help staff in selecting foster parents for the project. The facts and figures of books and journals about "good" foster parents faded as the integrity and wisdom of these four women pressed into the staff's experience. Their inherent knowledge of boundaries, developmental needs, and respect for the biological parents made us yearn for the day that cloning was a reality.

Such an endeavor, whether it be sponsoring a community luncheon or family interviews, requires administrative backing. Staff should argue that these kinds of ventures are ultimately cost-effective and can reduce no-shows. Administrators need to be aware that for many cultural groups "outpatient mental health" is culturally dystonic. Community events or family interviews diminish cultural dissonance and facilitate joining between agency and community.

This brings us to perhaps one of the hardest aspects of cross-cultural work: namely, knowing one's own culture.

THERAPIST, KNOW THY CULTURE

In order to go home, one must know how to get there. The first step is to develop a three-generation cultural genogram. What are the belief systems of the culture? What role assignments are dominant? How much does the family follow or conceal its cultural heritage? Given the therapist's sex and birth order, what role does that position fill within the culture? An eldest male son, for example, in the Indochinese culture, has some very specific expectations about duty to family, responsibility, and power in the family. What are the strengths, weaknesses, and biases of the culture? As the culture perceives them? As others perceive them? What is the culture's view about "helpers"? What is the culture's view of "outsiders"? What are the prejudices about other specific cultural groups (especially those the clinician is working with)?

The nature of these cultural influences is so often ingrained and subtle that most therapists are not aware of the impact on their work. As the Vietnamese say, "You can't see your nose because it's too close to your face." Let's take the opportunity to go back through the family album with a frame that lends a new light to old pictures.

REFERENCES

Deshpande, G. Translation and interpretation. *Opinion,* 1979, *20,* 1-3.

Geertz, C. *Myth, symbol, and culture.* New York: Norton, 1971.

Holmes, T.H. Holmes and Rahe Schedule of Recent Experience.

Lappin, J., & Scott, S. Intervention in a Vietnamese refugee family. In M. McGoldrick, J. Pearce, & J. Giordano (Eds.), *Ethnicity and family therapy.* New York: Guilford Press, 1982.

McGoldrick, M., Pearce, J., & Giordano, J. *Ethnicity and family therapy.* New York: Guilford Press, 1982.

Minuchin, S., & Fishman, C. *Family therapy techniques.* Cambridge, Mass.: Harvard University Press, 1981.

Montalvo, B. Home-school conflict and the Puerto Rican child. *Social Casework,* 1974, *55,* (2), 100-110.

Shon, P., & Ja, D. The Asian American family: A conceptual framework and psychotherapeutic approach. In M. McGoldrick, J. Pearce, & J. Giordano (Eds.), *Ethnicity and family therapy.* New York: Guilford Press, 1982.

Sluzki, C. Migration and family conflict. *Family Process,* 1979, *18*(4), 379-390.

10. Family Ethnography: A Tool for Clinicians

John Schwartzman, PhD
Assistant Professor
Center for Family Studies
The Family Institute of Chicago
Institute of Psychiatry
Northwestern Memorial Hospital
  and Northwestern University Medical School
Chicago, Illinois

BOTH FAMILY THERAPY AND CULTURAL ANTHROPOLOGY TRADI-
tionally have had as their subject matter small-scale, kin-oriented social
systems. Despite this and the recent interest in ethnicity (McGoldrick,
Pearce, & Giordano, 1982) in family theory, there has unfortunately been
little interaction between the two disciplines. This article is an attempt to
bridge these disciplines by using a perspective for understanding clinical
families similar to that anthropologists have traditionally used for the social
systems which have been their traditional subject matter. The goal is to
introduce the idea that family therapy can be understood as an ethnography,
or the study of sociocultural systems which calls for a slight shift in the usual
orientation of the clinician.

Just as the individual develops a unique personality learned within the
context of the family, each family integrates its sociocultural context into a
unique family culture. Culture provides a set of rules for individual behavior
in different relationships and contexts at various stages in the life cycle. All
cultures must produce individuals capable of both functioning in a group and
transmitting the cultural tradition to the next generation. More abstractly,
culture provides basic premises about the relationship of the self and its
social, biological, and ideological context. As a consequence of the structure of recurring context, individuals learn basic assumptions about "how
the world works." At a functional level, culture can also be viewed as a self-
regulating system. It can be understood as the meanings that individuals give
to the patterns of interaction that compose the social systems of which they
are a part.

Culture, as the "webs of significance"—beliefs and values—functions as
a homeostat, maintaining within limits the relationships between individuals
and their social context. It provides solutions that have been successful in the
past for relationships among individual families, social systems, and their
physical context. Culture is the most abstract system in which individuals
operate, so that cultural basic premises are extremely difficult to change but
crucial for any therapist to consider in attempting to intervene in the family
system.

In all societies, the most pervasive early context of learning is that of the
family, where infants' basic premises about themselves and about their
relationship to the context are learned. The structure and function of the
family must be such that its children develop basic premises or "habits of
thought" (Bateson, 1972) in "synch" with those of the sociocultural context of which the family is a part, so that they can function within it
appropriately.

An exotic example, Bali, illustrates this concept. In Balinese culture, which is perhaps the most formal and polite of any in the world, the rules of group behavior are emphasized at the expense of individuality (Mead & Bateson, 1942). At each stage of the life cycle, appropriate behaviors are reinforced while idiosyncratic aspects of the self are discouraged. This is an obvious contrast to the American middle class in which the autonomy, individuality, and achievement of the self is increasingly emphasized while that of the group, less so. This type of second-level learning (Bateson, 1972) is metaphorized as individual world view.

For example, in many achievement-oriented families—in which one is urged to work hard and do as well as possible in order to be rewarded—it can be hypothesized that the contingencies of interaction metaphorized as a world view would be "instrumental" in learning theory: One learns that one must compete and, if successful, will be rewarded. This can be contrasted to what would be deutero-learned in a "fatalistic" world whereby one learns not to compete for a possible reward but rather to accept whatever happens.

CULTURE AND LEVEL OF ABSTRACTION

The level of abstraction implicit in a cultural perspective has generally been ignored by family therapists (see Vogel & Bell, 1968; Jackson, 1970, for exceptions). Another exception to this is the work of Kluckhohn (1958) and Spiegel (1971), who have developed a number of ways to analyze the "value orientations" of people, which order their patterns of behavior and thought in all areas of activity. These value orientations provide the solution to a limited number of universal, abstract problems. Kluckhohn and Spiegel define the five problems crucial for all human groups: the character of the innate human nature, the relationship of humanity to nature, the temporal focus of human life, the modality of human activity, and the modality of human relationships to other humans. These universal problems and the orientations that each society adapts to solve them are useful comparatively as a "grid," since societies and subcultures can be categorized in terms of their solutions to these core problems. At the same time, this may be a misguided way for clinicians to utilize culture because it is at an inappropriate level of abstraction. Rather, the clinician should learn about a family's culture by interacting with the family. Learning about the Afro-American family, the Chinese American family, and so forth from a description of their typical characteristics may interfere with the therapist developing sensitivity to a particular family's culture.

LEARNING FAMILY CULTURE

To make sense of culture, one must learn it from the "inside out," making sense of the data provided or produced by a family rather than by a taxonomy from the "outside in," that is, a generalized classification of "typical" families of various ethnic groups or subcultures. Such labeling interferes with a careful diagnosis for each unique family culture. More important is awareness at a more abstract level of family "culture," however the particular family manifests it.

To describe the Mexican American family or the American Indian family, whose host countries have tens of millions of people and speak dozens of languages and have widely varying relationships within their American context, is no more useful for clinicians than is discussing the American family. This is especially true since there are so many ethnic variations and so many immigrant populations with various degrees of assimilation within and between groups.

For example, the author has seen a family in which the father was Jewish Irish and the mother was Korean American. The precipitating incident that brought them into therapy was the son's flunking out of a prestigious university and returning home. This enraged the mother. Moreover, she was also initiating a divorce due to her husband's obvious professional failure despite impressive academic credentials. The mother, having many academic credentials of her own, was much more successful than her husband. The weakness of men and the success of women permeated the histories of both families of origin. Knowledge about typical cultural patterns of Irish, Jewish, or Korean families would have only interfered with making sense of this family. Obviously, it had developed its own unique culture, focusing almost entirely on success and failure. Unraveling the various historical threads of its Korean-Jewish-Irish cultural background would have been useless except if used as part of a therapeutic intervention, for example, changing the locus of the problem to the culture, rather than the spouse. The therapist must remember that culture is embodied in the individual's belief system, it does not exist "out there," and thus must be sought in the family members, not in the therapist's beliefs about the culture of the family's ethnic group. For example, a number of Eastern European Jewish families seen by this author rather than being insight-oriented, affective, and verbal as described in the literature (McGoldrick, Pearce, & Giordano, 1982) had controlled affect, were concrete thinkers, and were not particularly verbal.

Another family seen in therapy by the author was North Indian. Both spouses were Christian and professionals and extremely conflictual. It was completely dissimilar from another family, an Indian American family in which the father was a nonpracticing Hindu, and his wife was an American Catholic, and both were disappointed in each other's failing to meet their mutual needs. This pattern also differed from an extended Indian family seen in therapy in which both spouses were nominally Hindu and extremely conflictual about their relative status. In these three families, their unique blends of family dynamics, their cultural origins, and their current cultural context were inseparable and only meaningful when acted out in family interaction, that is, whether or not they were typical was irrelevant to that particular family's problem and its solution.

The therapist must be able to "hear" the family culture and that of its more inclusive sociocultural context at many levels of organization and abstraction through the dysfunctional family member's own cultural categories in order to intervene successfully. The clinician must not try to force the family into categories that the clinician feels should be appropriate for the subculture to which it belongs. This includes the rules and contingencies of interaction that are acted out and communicated in many modes at many levels of organization and abstraction (e.g., verbal and nonverbal communication, dress, neighborhood, etc.).

A family diagnosis should include the cultural context, the family's relationship to its immediate social context, and the world view of individual family members, all revealed in intrafamilial communications about family members' basic premises. These together create a family ethnography, analogous to work done by anthropologists studying more inclusive social systems. For the clinician, feedback on the diagnosis is immediately available, provided by whether or not the symptomatic behavior can be understood as an attempted solution for the individual and the family within their social context. Attempted interventions by the therapist also provide feedback for the diagnosis in terms of structure and basic premises.

In family or systems therapy, a most important diagnostic question is: What is the meaning of that which is communicated so that recurring patterns of structure at different levels of organization and abstraction are maintained or changed? More specifically, there are a number of questions the therapist should be able to answer, because the problem or symptom and the responses to it are crucial comments on "dissonances" in the structure and basic premises of the system in question (see Haley, 1963, 1976). More specific diagnostic questions are: How does this symptomatic dysfunctional behavior "make sense" in terms of dissonances in the structure and basic premises of the individual's social context, and those encountered in the past? and What are the beliefs of family members about themselves and each other that maintain and are maintained by the structure of the system?

These concepts are illustrated in the interaction of a first-generation Jewish couple, raised in a Jewish neighborhood in Los Angeles. Both sets of parents lost many relatives to the Nazis. Their parents strongly reinforced the notion of the dangers of the Gentile world and the necessity of depending on oneself and fellow Jews against basically antagonistic Gentiles. This couple had moved to the Midwest and lived in an Irish neighborhood, which was extremely alienating and lonesome for the couple. As the husband stated, "I don't have anyone I can wave my arms around at and argue with." After the birth of their twins, the couple created a recurring oscillating cycle of conflict (much more intense than their previous loud but quickly forgotten arguments) and distance. This resulted in a series of anxiety attacks by the husband when he felt too distant and isolated, and he then experienced panic. This was followed by his wife trying to calm him down, reducing the distance, thus beginning the conflictual aspect of the cycle again. Consequently, various aspects of this family's particular functioning were exacerbated by a number of larger cultural issues concerning the dangers of being Jewish in a non-Jewish context. Their basic premises were based on the metaphor of the world as conflictual, with the Jews against everybody else.

ETHNOGRAPHY AS DIAGNOSIS

A good family ethnography will reveal the basic premises of the family—those assumptions or rules for contingencies of interaction that are never questioned or conscious and are so abstract that they are self-validating (Bateson, 1972). They are acted out at the level of the individual and the family and are validated by beliefs, rituals, and myths about individuals and by more general cultural values. This includes patterns of what people say and do about what they say and do (i.e., multiple levels of organization and abstraction) and ways in which the meanings of that which is communicated maintain the structure of a social system or push it toward change. The therapist must be sensitive to the family's choice of modes or codes, the content of its interactions, and its values and beliefs, all of which compose the "family culture" maintained by myths (Ferreira, 1958) and the ideology of the family.

Since the symptom is a 'comment on" dissonances in the family, and an attempt to maintain these dissonances within tolerable limits, then the basic premises of the families and the family structure that maintains and is maintained by them must be revealed in the symptoms and its responses in a self-regulating process (Weakland, Fisch, Watzlawick, & Bodin, 1974).

CULTURE AS A FAMILY METAPHOR

All communication is metaphoric in that something is being communicated in terms of something else. Each family has a particular mode or modes to communicate, that is, some communicate positive affect by giving things, some do it verbally, some do it physically, and some with food. Different cultures express it different ways, but each family develops their own idiosyncratic manner. Concurrently, each family develops myths that rationalize and validate their ways of doing things, for example, "We Smiths have always been gregarious, unable to handle liquor, good cooks, and so forth."

At a less inclusive level, family members' world views are metaphors for the contingencies between self and social context, learned in their families of origin and acted out and validated in other contexts. The dysfunction, dysphoria, or symptom within this context as described by Haley (1976) can be understood as an attempted solution to the dissonances at the various levels of the social systems within which the individual is presently oriented, or in relation to those levels within which interaction took place in the past in terms of deutero-learned basic premises. Cultural dissonances and familial dissonances can be viewed as analogues at different levels of organization and abstraction. An example can be seen in a syndrome that is a metaphor for the dissonances that are manifestations of the Protestant Ethic, a basic cultural premise in our society, that has been amplified to toxic levels. Individual hard work becomes a spiritual end which beyond certain levels results in driven Type A behavior and at times physical illness. This behavior is maintained by a world view stating, "The harder you strive, the better."

A North Indian client and his American wife came into therapy with the author because of marital problems. Mr. A's major complaint was that his wife was not nurturing and empathic. Mrs. A came from a somewhat emotionally undemonstrative and distant family, and stated that she felt that Mr. A was too demanding and hypochondriacal and was angry that he was demanding care while he was not supportive and appreciative of her.

> Mr. A stated that he always tried to help others, but always felt resentful because they inevitably disappointed him because they never reciprocated in a way he felt was adequate. His family of origin was characterized by a number of longstanding, unresolved conflicts and resulting coalitions among his siblings. He was a double refugee, first from what was Pakistan to India, and then from India to the United States. He believed that being disappointed and the resulting storing up of resentments was both a familial and a North Indian trait.

What must be resolved is this dissonance; its etiology in Indian versus American culture is irrelevant to its solution. More important for the clinician is to perceive each individual's basic premises or world view and utilize them as levers for change.

QUESTIONING THE THERAPIST'S PREMISES

Another important aspect of an ethnographical approach to family therapy is the assumption that the basic premises of the therapist are understood as one belief system, rather than as the appropriate belief system. This should be especially clear when it is obvious that the family's culture is different from the therapist's. The therapist's beliefs, like those of the family, are only a "comment on" the cultural context where they were learned, rather than the truth.

Ideally, this should make therapists question their basic premises concerning assumptions about family life that are generally unquestioned, such as a high degree of intimacy between spouses, the nuclear family, and so forth, all viewed unquestionably as positive. Haley (1976) has perhaps done the most to confront certain basic premises of therapists, such as the universally positive therapeutic effect of the clear communication of all affect.

Traditionally, at least, family therapists were often not self-reflexive about their own basic premises, instead making them the unquestioned template for appropriate behavior, and belief in terms of appropriate sex roles, expression of affect, intimacy, and family structure. In contrast, ethnographers were forced into their awareness that their informants were from obviously different cultures, and were not "patients," so the informants' basic premises were not dismissed as pathological or inferior, just different. The whole thrust of anthropology was to describe and understand these different ways of living.

AN ABDUCTIVE APPROACH

Another main difference between anthropology and other social sciences is methodological. Anthropology, at least traditionally, did not employ an experimental methodology, but rather intense observation and data gathering with vaguer ideas concerning method. Consequently, instead of using an inductive approach (in which "facts" are gathered, and hypotheses are validated or proved false), or the deductive approach of mathematics or logic, anthropology uses what has been termed abduction (Bateson, 1972). Abduction can, in fact, be understood as a clinical methodology. Rather than measuring, abduction is classifying by analogy or metaphor wherein something is seen as an example under a case—for example, these symptoms (fever, red spots) indicate this illness, these behaviors and these statements indicate this world view, and so forth. It is a way of devising theories in order to explain groups of facts. For anthropology, it was an attempt to explain disparate phenomena in strange cultures as elements in some more inclusive classification so that some aspect of this culture is understood: That is, how does this unusual behavior fit together with other strange behaviors in a cultural whole?

This "fitting together" should lead to the diagnostic question: what context of learning would make this perception and this behavior an adaptive response to this context? For each family member, the therapist should ask the questions: What is the world view of this family member that makes this behavior make sense in this context? and What is the evidence from what they communicate about each other, about themselves, and the family?

CULTURE AS REVEALED IN RITUALS, SYMPTOMS, AND MYTHS

The difficulty with doing a family ethnography, as in doing a traditional ethnography, is that the most basic premises and cultural patterns and values are generally out of awareness of those having them so that they are often not consciously revealed by family members. However, there are two situations when these generally unquestioned, accepted premises are highlighted and brought into consciousness or at least made more obvious to the clinician or the ethnographer. These can be as readily perceived in families as in cultures. In both contexts, these premises are revealed in certain types of rituals: calendrical rites, those rituals celebrated at particular times during the year, and rites of passage, those rituals commemorating changes in the life cycle (or, in terms of dysfunctional families, their failure to make these changes). Geertz (1973) describes rituals as models of and models for. In the family rituals of both kinds, calendrical rites and rites of passage, the social organization of the family is acted out. In the performance of any ritual, a model for appropriate structure is made explicit so that the basic premises are revealed.

The first type of ritual mentioned above, calendrical rites, celebrated either at the same time or to commemorate a yearly event, validates the basic premises and social structure of the system that performs them. All rituals must be acted out or participated in to be effective. Those who act them out validate the basic premises and structure of the social system of which the ritual is a model of and a model for (Geertz, 1973). In families these are often civil or religious holidays, birthdays, or anniversaries. The most basic aspect of the social structure is revealed in who is in attendance. Being a member of the family often requires attendance at these rituals, or an "excuse" for being absent. One's role in the ritual also reveals various aspects of the social culture. As in any ritual, its "unquestionable" nature provides it with its power, analogous to the "sacred" in religion (see Rappaport, 1971). Who is in attendance and each participant's role in the performance of the ritual validate family structure. Its violation—due to appropriate changes expected at various times in the life cycle or symptomatic behavior—is highlighted during calendrical family rituals; these then are comments on current family culture.

Families often appear in therapy at exactly those times when people traditionally perform rituals: either during periods in the life cycle where change is supposed to take place (e.g., onset of puberty, leaving home, adulthood, marriage, or death) or when unresolved dissonances are amplified and threaten to alter the system (e.g., divorce, birth, or death) or when these changes have taken place and the family is in a resulting crisis.

The onset of symptomatic behavior is a close analogue to rites of passage except in contrast to rituals, symptoms by their paradoxical nature prevent these culturally appropriate changes from taking place. Diagnostically, symptoms, like rituals, are "comments on" the dissonances that threaten the system of which they are a part. Their content, expressed in a particular code or mode, is also a comment about the family's basic premises. Consequently, the symptom is a "kernel" of meaning that reveals an attempted adaptive response to the basic premises of the system, by necessity in the core language or code of the family.

For example, the Katz family, in which both parents were second-generation Jewish Americans from Eastern Europe, was extremely invested in the children's education. Both Mr. and Mrs. Katz stated that they themselves were poor students and were going to give their children every scholastic advantage, such as private schools, tutors, and so forth. The middle child, aged 7, was described as having a mild learning disability, was extremely bright, but was also behaviorally out of control and in danger of being expelled from the special school he was attending. This situation brought the family into therapy. The parents said they would go to any lengths to help their children be successful in school, but recognized that their son had a learning disability and questioned how successful he could actually be irrespective of what they did. They were also sure he would destroy the office.

The father was an extremely successful, but disorganized business-man who in some years earned hundreds of thousands of dollars, but saved little. He bought extremely expensive items for everybody in the family, including himself, but always put himself in financial difficulties and was not able to invest any of his income. The family was completely disorganized. The parents set no consistent limits on their son, and the children fought constantly without parental intervention, did not respect closed doors (including their parents' bedroom), and did not respect one another's personal property. The father often came home extremely tired, blamed his wife for the children's behavior, and bribed them not to bother him.

The mother in this family stated that she was the chauffeur and babysitter and resented the husband's lack of involvement. She said her husband bought off the kids because he did not want another job when he came home from work, so she had to raise the children herself. She said that she needed help with their son and could not do it herself. She also stated that she believed that it was a family problem. (The school psychologist had recommended family therapy.) Consequently, this child's symptom served its usual homeostatic function of bringing the parents together by making it necessary for father to be involved with controlling his son and going to family therapy. At the same time it highlighted a number of basic premises and values of the family. The most obvious was that school problem which brought the family into therapy. It appeared that education of the children (an important value in Jewish culture) was communicated by their concern regarding this symptom.

At a more abstract level, the parents communicated a world view of a universe characterized by a lack of constraint, one aspect of which was the assumption that people were out of control and "acted on" by events in their context. Father was unable to stop his spending and said money "flowed like water through his fingers." He practiced what he termed "brinksmanship" in his business, saving nothing, borrowing large sums. His father was a professional gambler, who was gambling on his death-bed to leave his family with a big stake. His mother supported him well into adulthood, because she knew he "couldn't follow a budget." His wife was always described as weak and incompetent by her own parents and her husband. She stated she married her husband because he was extremely generous and "nice" to her. Consequently, the symptom of lack of control, and at a more concrete level, school failure, can be seen as highlighting this family's basic premises about themselves and more generally a world view characterized by a lack of constraint, meta-phorized at many levels in their lives.

At another level of abstraction, myths validate and maintain basic prem-ises. These unquestioned, unverifiable beliefs about individuals and the family maintain the status quo by transferring dissonances from patterns of interaction "inside" individuals, to more inclusive social organizations, and by this mechanism they also function as regulators for the entire family. For example, the family mentioned above can be seen as utilizing certain myths to maintain their structure. As stated earlier, the young boy defined as out of control, functioned in a context where his parents did not set any limits on him. In addition, the father stated that he himself, when growing up, was mostly truant from school to play pool. When asked what his parents did about his truancy, he said, "Nothing." After his father's death, his mother continued to send him money. Clearly, lack of constraint, acted out through problems in school and general irresponsibility, was a family theme for several generations. Early in the treatment, when the relationship between the parents' inconsistent constraints and consequences and their son's inap-propriate behavior was being pointed out, the mother suddenly stated, "You know, I probably had a learning disability too," to explain her own lack of school success and to validate their behaviors with their son—demonstrating the power of myth about self.

CONCLUSION

A good family diagnosis must include the culture of the family and individual members' world views within the social context of which it is a part. By paying closer attention to the "raw" data (although always con-tingent on the perceiver's world view), the culture of the family will be revealed. The social organization is acted out in a rule-governed pattern, while the beliefs that maintain it and the mode in which it is expressed can be viewed as core aspects of family culture. These are also maintained by myths about the family and its members that both explain and maintain their behaviors. Rituals in which participation validates the social order are another means by which the family system is maintained and its culture is revealed. Having an awareness of the ways by which a family manifests its unique culture facilitates the effectiveness of intervention. The therapist who is sensitive to the family's culture has a broader repertoire of interventions to draw upon.

REFERENCES

Bateson, G. *Steps to an ecology of mind*. New York: Ballantine, 1972.

Ferreira, A. Family myth and homeostasis. *Archives of General Psychiatry*, 1958, *9*, 457-463.

Geertz, C. *Interpretation of cultures*. New York: Basic Books, 1973.

Haley, J. *Strategies of psychotherapy*. New York: Grune & Stratton, 1963.

Haley, J. *Problem-solving therapy*. San Francisco: Jossey-Bass, 1976.

Jackson, D. The study of the family. In N. Ackerman (Ed.), *Family process*. New York: Basic Books, 1970.

Kluckhohn, F. Variations in the basic values of family systems. *Social Casework*, 1958, *39*, 63-72.

McGoldrick, M., Pearce, J., & Giordano, J. *Ethnicity and family therapy*. New York: Guilford Press, 1982.

Mead, M., & Bateson, G. *Balinese character*. New York: New York Academy of Sciences, 1942.

Rappaport, R. Ritual, sanctity, and cybernetics. *American Anthropologist*, 1971, *73*, 59-76.

Spiegel, J. *Transactions: The interplay between individual, family, and society*. New York: Science House, 1971.

Vogel, E., & Bell, N. The emotionally disturbed child as family scapegoat. In N. Bell & E. Vogel (Eds.), *A modern introduction to the family*. New York: Free Press, 1968.

Weakland, J., Fisch, R., Watzlawick, P., & Bodin, A. Brief therapy: Focus problem resolution. *Family Process*, 1974, *13*, 141-168.